Girlie Collectibles

Putting a price on $exism

PINUP CALENDAR, 1960s. $10.

NUTCRACKER, 13" tall, carved wood, souvenir from the Philippines, 1950s. $27.50.

BALLERINA, 36" tall, carved and polychromed wood with net tutu, 1940s. $1,500.

Also by Leland & Crystal Payton:

Scientific Collectibles

Space Toys: A Collector's Guide to Science Fiction and Astronautical Toys

Turned On: Decorative Lamps of the Fifties

Branson: Country Themes and Neon Dreams

The Insider's Guide to Branson
(with Kate Klise)

Patio Daddy-O: '50s Recipes with a '90s Twist
(with Gideon Bosker and Karen Brooks)

Girlie Collectibles

Politically Incorrect Objets d'Art

Leland & Crystal Payton
Photographs by Leland Payton

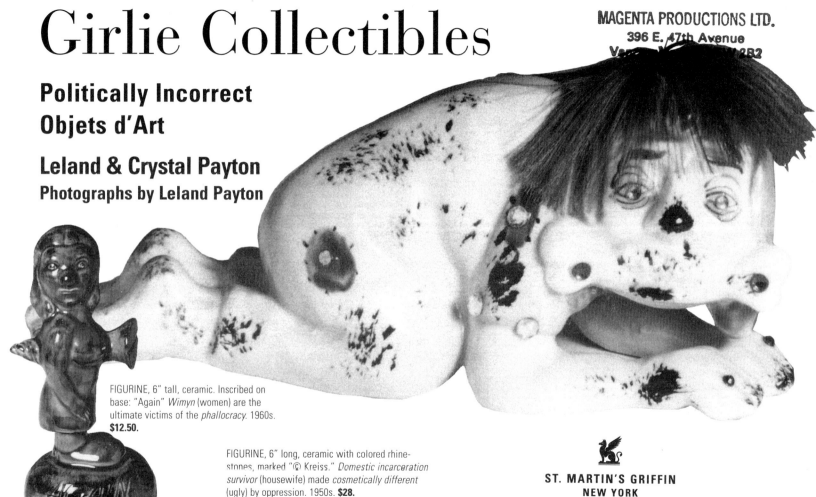

FIGURINE, 6" tall, ceramic. Inscribed on base: "Again" *Wimyn* (women) are the ultimate victims of the *phallocracy*. 1960s. **$12.50.**

FIGURINE, 6" long, ceramic with colored rhinestones, marked "© Kreiss." *Domestic incarceration survivor* (housewife) made *cosmetically different* (ugly) by oppression. 1950s. **$28.**

ST. MARTIN'S GRIFFIN
NEW YORK

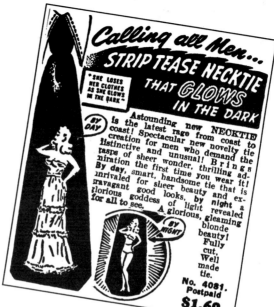

GIRLIE COLLECTIBLES: POLITICALLY INCORRECT OBJETS D'ART

Design by Plug Nickel Productions, Springfield, MO

Library of Congress Cataloging-in-Publication Data

Payton, Crystal.
    Girlie collectibles : politically incorrect objets d'art / by Crystal and Leland Payton.
        p.   cm.
    ISBN: 0-312-14532-2
    1. Girlie collectibles--United States--Catalogs. I. Payton, Leland. II. Title.
    NK5090.p39 1996
    704.9'424'0973--dc20   96-21447
                                                  CIP

First St. Martin's Griffin Edition: October 1996

10 9 8 7 6 5 4 3 2 1

Contents

Introduction

When the politically correct have silenced offensive words and terms from the lips of college students there will remain a vast quantity of material similar to the stuff in this book. It will be harder to eliminate, as it is found in the flea markets, antique shows, attics, basements, china cabinets and yard sales of America. If this bric-a-brac and kitsch can be gathered and converted to landfill, there remain the museums and fine estates of Europe. There, efforts to destroy their older, heavier and more valuable yard ornaments and wall hangings that are *inappropriate*, *hostile* or *demeaning* to the politically correct will be met, the authors feel, with considerably more resistance.

VENUS IN SHELL, 18" high, cast alabaster, Hennecke's Florentine Statuary, Milwaukee, 1888. The *DWEMs* (dead white European males) who preferred such *lookist* decorative objects were not *fatophobic* (fearful of obesity). Today's value: **$375.**

Woman's form has been utilized, co-opted, stolen, appropriated for centuries. Some of the intentions were religious or magical; some esthetic or decorative; some downright mean-spirited. Some of this residual imagery of women is universally regarded as priceless. Some other artifacts depicting women are regarded by many as worthless. In today's politically correct atmosphere, the prudent collector might be well advised not to display his/her better kitsch in public as it may create a *hostile social environment.*

6

The Great Mother

1. GODDESS OF FERTILITY, carved stone, Iran, 4th century B.C. **Priceless.**

2. LIQUOR DECANTER, 10" high, ceramic. Marked "Pat M6947." Head comes off to pour. Missing cups. 1950s. **$25.**

3. STATUE OF DEMETER, terra cotta, Greece, 5th century B.C. **Priceless.**

Good Girls . . .

SERVING TRAY, 10" x 13", lithographed tin. "Betty Tray," advertises Coca-Cola. (Incidentally, Coke did contain cocaine in its earliest, most "refreshing" years). 1914. **$500.**

SERVING TRAY, 10" x 13", lithographed tin. 1924. **$400.**
NOTE: These are both original trays. Many Coke trays have been reproduced. Be sure it's original before paying high prices.

& Bad Girls Sell

The image of women, it was discovered early on, attracts attention to manufactured products. Sometimes it is seemingly innocent, as in the old Coke trays. Other *lookist* exploitations of *wimyn* (women) advance *least good* (bad) habits.

HAREM BEAUTIES ART KNIVES. This cut shows a sales board outift, a gambling device in which you paid 5 cents to punch out one of the holes. If the piece of paper you poked out matched the number, you got the prize. Circa 1920. Individual knives today: **$40.**

CIGARETTE AD, 1914. **$10.**

On Collecting

Even before we became aware of political correctness, in our travels as migratory antique dealers we began picking up junk and kitsch that had a condescending, satiric, even insulting tone – some of it intentional, some not. This book is the outcome of our archaeology in attics, basements, garage sales, malls, and flea markets. America used to be a lot funnier place and this is what this stuff, to us, basically proves.

On Prices

For the most part the prices we quote are the prices we found on the objects in markets and malls. As with any market information, it is subject to variation from place to place.

In the past, we have done books on *Scientific Collectibles*, *Space Toys*, and 1950s lamps. We have authored dozens of articles on other antiques and collectibles. Often the subjects of our books and articles dramatically increased in price. Maybe coincidence, or maybe we knew what we were talking about. Time will tell.

CANE HANDLE, "White Metal Leg in silver and bronze finish mounted as handle on good quality wood cane." Gellman Bros. Wholesale Premium Merchandise & Novelties, 1929. Originally they cost 80 cents a dozen. Today's value: **$18/each.**

You Be the Judge

We live in an era in which image is, for many (especially the politically correct), the only reality. There is by no means agreement between the various sects of the ultrasensitive thought- and speech-police, but they all have a near-fanatical need to be the sole source of their own image.

As a group similar to radicals of other era – Jacobins, Marxist-Leninists, Maoists, and other repressive and humorless radicals – they view *male-stream* (mainstream) Western society, with its admittedly mixed successes in science, art, literature, technology, and politics, as an exploitive force to be deconstructed and overthrown.

The authors disagree . . . and our *DWEM* (dead white European male) authored Constitution, with its First Amendment, does *empower* us to offer this fragment of the *Euro-American world-view*. Crystal can assure you that it is not exclusively an *ego-testicle worldview*.

JUDGE HUMOR MAGAZINE, 1929. **$15.**

11

The Shy Young Man

POSTCARD, printed in England circa 1910. **$3.**

STATUE, 8" tall, bisque.
Paper label says: "Hand painted
Lenwile AA Ardalt Artware Japan."
1960s. **$17.50.**

"IT'S A SHAME TO TAKE THE MONEY"

SOUVENIR ST. LOUIS WORLD'S FAIR, 1904

PIN TRAY, 5" long, aluminum. Souvenir of the St.. Louis
World's Fair, 1904. "It's a shame to take the money," mut-
ters the *pre-patriarchal shoeshine person* after directing
his *male gaze* at an *objectified female other*. A tender
moment in the development of a chauvinist. **$35.**

They're everywhere ...they're everywhere!

The stolen images of *wimyn* (women) have been *economically exploited* throughout the *Euro-American capitalistic world.* High and low – from auctions at Sotheby's to flea markets and garage sales – you can find these *appropriated multi-offensive* images and objects. Seek and ye shall find. For a price you can amass your own collection. Bargain if you can. You may turn a profit later . . . as so many before you have.

floozie

Broad

TART

fox

Baby Doll

CHEESECAKE

T 'n A

pussycat

Dame

Bitch

skirt

Bimbo

Chick

honey

wench

INCENSE BURNER, 6" tall, painted cast metal. Artist signed, "R Janny" on front of pillow. Turn of the century. Figure lifts up to reveal the space to put the incense. **$345.**

1. China Dolls and Pot Metal Tarts
The Slang Theory of Flea Market Women

HEAD VASES, high fired ceramic, 1950s. These are highly collectible today. $27-$49.50.

"The best slang is not only ingenious and amusing: it also embodies a kind of social criticism. It not only provides new names for a series of everyday concepts, some new and some old; it also says something about them . . . the vocabulary of the vulgar is likely to be larger, in proportion to the total vocabulary, than that of the cultured and it is harder working."
  – H. L. Mencken, *The American Language*, 1919

This ingenious and exuberant stuff, these flea market babes, is to staid middle-class decorative accessories as slang is to formal language. It is zippy, often novel, never boring, and frequently embodies a kind of social criticism, like slang. It's vernacular made visible. It is artifactual argot, made by a people who are naturally rebellious and irreverent. It is cant cast in plaster, molded in plastic, printed on pulp. Cheap and cheeky, cocky, flip, fresh, lippy, nervy, smart-assed Slang Americana.

"Slang is a form of colloquial speech created in a spirit of defiance and aiming at freshness and novelty . . . Its figures are consciously farfetched and are intentionally drawn from the most ignoble of sources, closely akin to profanity in its spirit, its aim is to shock." George H. McKnight, 1923
Slang Americana's most defiant, fresh, novel,

ignoble, profane and shocking choice of theme may be women. Wonderfully punful and extremely objectionable treasures can be dug up in flea markets. Indeed, high art and the proper decorative arts have long utilized the female form – to the now-shrill protests of feminists.

This volume is devoted to women's image, but Slang Americana is universal and we have more subjects in the works. Gender and race are eternal battlegrounds. Skirmishes between men and women and ethnic and cultural groups cross political and geographic boundaries, leaving a rich artifactual record. We plan for men, the creators of all this grief, a *larger than standard size* (fat) tome of their own. Race and ethnicity will follow.

While the furor over environmental and animal rights issues is more recent in origin, it too has its shrill, humorless, "the sky is falling" zealots with the same will to domination that characterizes radical feminism ('scuse me, gender feminism) and militant multi-cults . . . and the flea markets and vintage clothing shops are loaded with remnants of *non-human animals* like alligator purses, taxidermied squirrels holding beer cans and chromolithograph ads showing factories belching the black 19th-century smoke of progress. So we welcome them to the fray.

Pointy-headed people have never liked the plain speech of ordinary Americans. They have dogged Mark Twain, waging a hundred year war to have "Huck Finn" taken off library shelves. Not only do they disdain unregulated and vulgar language, they have thought themselves superior to the Kewpie dolls, skeleton rings with ruby eyes, duck TV lamps, LA-Z-BOYS with gold sparkles embedded in the plastic, yard ornaments with Victorian versions of nymphs, bird baths held up by bullfrogs, chopped Day-Glo hot rods, monster trucks, land-locked restaurants in the shape of riverboats or any of the other exuberant artifacts created for and by the vulgate taste of pure, 100% unadulterated democracy. Since the Puritans, the censoring class-es have waged an unrelenting war against such raw expressions of the New World character and its often raucous sensibilities.

Like American slang, this stuff reflects the tawdry imagination, sarcastic humor and moxie of its cre-ators and consumers. Slang Americana is the 3-D version of everything a speech code prohibits. It is cliché cast in pot metal, stereotype set in ceramic, parody molded in plastic. For clichés are always with us and stereotypes have some faint echo of truth. And we have all, boys and girls, black and white, red and yellow, old and young, been pilloried or pictured at one time or another by the insolence of Slang Americana.

Although the politically correct are quick to charge discrimination, Slang Americana is an equal opportunity offender of gender, race, and any other area of hypersensitivity. Any *melanin-impoverished* or *melanin-enhanced wofem* can get her tit in a wringer (or accordion). We've seen the Mammy ashtray newly cloned as a large limited edition cookie jar priced at $450.

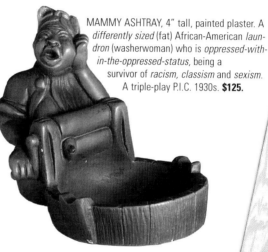

MAMMY ASHTRAY, 4" tall, painted plaster. A *differently sized* (fat) African-American *laun-dron* (washerwoman) who is *oppressed-with-in-the-oppressed-status*, being a survivor of *racism, classism* and *sexism*. A triple-play P.I.C. 1930s. **$125.**

COMIC POSTCARD, 9" long, card-board, "Made in Japan." On back it says: "Komic Kard, It's a Post Card! It's a Plak!" The prudent contemporary *sadistic sexist* would be well advised neither to mail nor to hang this card in his work environment. 1950s. **$3.**

KNIGHT RADIO AND LETTER OPENER, 11½" tall, metal figure on plastic radio case. "Made in Japan." 1960s.
$26.

Besides being fresh and original, the spirit of American slang (and its artifactual equivalents) is sometimes admittedly *insensitive* and may make some delicate souls *uncomfortable.*

"Slang always tends toward degradation rather than elevation . . . much of our slang purposely expresses amorality, cynicism, and toughness . . . Many use slang just because it is not standard or polite. Many use slang to show their rebellion against *boobs, fuddy-duddies, marks* and *squares* . . . Because it is not standard, formal or acceptable under all conditions slang is usually considered vulgar, impolite or boorish." *Dictionary of American Slang,* Harold Wentworth and Stuart Berg Flexner, eds. 1975

Who is the P.C. Crowd and why will this stuff make them *uncomfortable?*

Enter the Politically Correct, a group not content merely to write long-winded treatises denouncing the bad taste of the public (washing our collective mouths out with soap) but preferring to make a crime out of the admittedly raunchy tradition of popular taste. They are radicals posing as moderates to gain sympathy and get their way. Now, like a horse with the bit in its teeth, they're running wild.

They are a litigious group. As a child might run wailing to Mommy when Johnny picks on her at the playground, so do the Politically Correct run to Big Nanny Court System with each and every gripe. As anyone today who has listened to the radio, watched TV, read a newspaper, gone to school, or had a job knows – you'd better watch your p's and q's or a lawsuit might ensue. The "too-good-for-this-or-any-other-world" crowd of the past wrote tracts and rapped knuckles, but the Politically Correct (hereafter referred to as the P.C). take names and kick ass.

Political incorrectness today covers a broad band of conventional experience. Bob Hope's half century of USO shows with leggy starlets can be seen as exploitation ("I just want you to see what you're

Cockocratic hero: "an idolized and widely imitated snool, one who serves as a sacred role model in patriarchy, the State of Atrocity."

Mary Daly lists three examples of the *cockocratic hero:* the Marquis de Sade, Daniel Boone, Jack the Ripper. Even the more widely accepted great men don't get off easy: Washington, the Father of our Country, was a slave owner; Lincoln's Gettysburg Address is, in Mary Daly's judgement, bull; and Beethoven wrote music that could inspire rape. Even *Uncle Sham* (Uncle Sam) is said to personify the *american Stag-nation.*

And how has the *phallocracy* accomplished this through the eons? The primary weapon in the arsenal of subjugation is language.

If the numerous writers' guidelines and grammars of the politically correct can rage on, page after page, trying to delete the feared and hated three letter word "man" from human, woman, mankind, mannequin, manpower, patrolman, fisherman, fireman, and the thousand other gender-biased *Manglish* (English) words, imagine their bent out of shape, burned up, fit to be tied, huffy, mad as a wet hen, peeved and pissed off responses to the rich vocabulary of slang from which sensibilities this stuff came.

They have their work cut out for them.

"Male supremacy is fused into the language, so that every sentence both heralds and affirms it , , , as Prometheus stole fire from the gods, so feminists will have to steal the power of naming from men." *Andrea Dworkin, 1979.*

Marriage is, to p.c. feminists, *patriarchal bondage.*

fighting for.") Families in suburbia trying to maintain Christmas traditions or live in the "right" school district are found *wanting in sensitivity.* NFL cheerleaders are now rarely scanned by TV, cameras as they dance, bounce, and lead the crowd – because that would be *sexist exploitation.*

Believing in neither God nor the Constitution (forces which somewhat restrained the earlier Puritans and their blue-nosed descendants), the P.C. Police, whose prophets are Marx and Mao, whose methods are absolutist and antidemocratic and whose vision is apocalyptic are ranging the land, moving beyond the groves of academe into business, city governments, and newspaper-style books. They are bent on eradicating words, thoughts, actions that make them *uncomfortable.* Certainly the sight of naked girls adorning ashtrays, secretary swatters, cavemen, and lamps made from deers' hooves, to name but a few, may assault their tender sensibilities even more.

We live in a material world. Stuff surrounds us. Not all of it is as silent, inanimate, uncommunicative as a coffee pot, toaster or bookshelf. Common objects can speak of distant times, other places, other people. The hypersensitive could go apoplectic in the attics of America, go ballistic in a flea market. We are born, live, and die in a material world – and we present to you some very material girls.

20

Political correctness assails that assumption. P.C. lives in a utopian world of an unrealizable future. It is made of feelings, opinions, attitudes, and talk – things not fired from common clay, wrought from base metal or stamped on the *flattened, processed carcasses of trees* (paper).

When Marxism, as a viable software for running a nation or economy, crashed, a lot of people who like to feel morally superior, not work too hard and tell everybody else what to do quickly rose from its ashes. Political correctness, to rework Veblen, is a result of the Leisure of the Theory Class. It should not be confused with the laudable efforts of earlier liberal concerns to improve society.

P.C. has flourished most notably in the People's Republic of China and the women and black studies departments of prestigious American universities. Deconstructionist English departments and revisionist history departments are also notorious lily-livered P.C.ers. Big foundations just can't get enough leftist, censorious anti-American chic as well.

"Using words as political weapons is a mind-stretching exercise. We recommend it."

Stereotypes, Distortions, and Omissions in U.S. History Textbooks, The Council on Interracial books for Children, Racism & Sexism Resource Center for Education, 1977.

War is a particularly objectionable activity of the *pops of patriarchy* (men) . . . it is "the male's normal method of compensation for not being female, namely, getting his Big Gun off . . . "
(Valerie Solinas, 1968.)

POSTCARD, 1943. **$3.**

MATCHBOOK, 1940s. **$3.**

P.C. vocabulary is the ultimate "Just Say No." It exhibits the overwhelming desire to bring everything down, to swallow it all in a black hole of negativity. It is artless, heartless romanticism. It has a "stop-the-world-I-want-to-get-off" quality, a deep desire for a state enforced heaven on earth. Guess who wears the wings.

That the P.C. crowd has taken such a strong foothold in academia and business is a tribute to the basic tolerance of the American public. "Why, golly gee, maybe you're right about that word. I don't want to hurt someone's feelings." Tolerance and the get-along nature of American may be our Achilles heel. What many Americans don't see is the wily will to domination of the P.C.ers and their desire to dictate "right speak, right think."

The end product of P.C.ness we figure will be a passionless, neutered, beige person with ill-defined features, a soft voice and limited vocabulary possibly resembling the creatures in "Close Encounters of the Third Kind," who feels no pain. In the P.C. Paradise they will be completely free of all the old hardships, conflicts, and disappointments that characterize human history and present-day reality. Apart from the obvious suspicion most of us have that the harder road is inescapable, the question arises: Even if achievable, who would really want the P.C. Paradise? We'll go with Mark Twain:

"Heaven for the climate, Hell for the company."

Think of Political Correctness as a fourth-rate, one-ring circus with no lions, no beautiful women in tights on the high wire, no cotton candy. Grotesque academic contortionists, talentless but vain, wander among mirthless, unpainted clowns. The shrill, preachy rhetoric of political barkers proclaims the pitiful assemblage to be not only the Greatest Show on Earth, but the only show on Earth. For the multi-cult tent shelters a one world, mono-cult, no-fun ideal. The price of a ticket is freedom. Welcome to eternal boredom under the P.C. Big Top.

Much as the P.C.ers like to think of themselves as cutting edge social engineers, our *her*story is rife with reformers, social critics, utopians, schoolmarms and preachers, all hell-bent on housebreaking the renegade, fencing the free ranger, reining in the roughnecks. They advocated such constraints as table manners, baths, no spitting on the sidewalks and Prohibition, in an effort to tame the land and *snivilize* its *snools*. We have no argument with some of this. At its best political correctness is proper, polite parlor parlance. In the larger context of communication and literature, it is stifling, boring, and unworkable.

Slang is a special language. It is a quick, easy, personal mode of speech which comes from jargon (shop talk, the technical even secret, vocabulary of a sub-group), argot (the cant and jargon of a criminal group). It is natural, often spontaneous. Probably few peoples enjoy the inexpensive, expressive objects that embody slang's cut-to-the-chase approach more than Americans do – as the contents of this book illustrate.

P.C. jargon, on the other hand, is full of negative euphemism, a "lingua non franca," both defensive and aggressive in nature. Slang generally simplifies things. It's shorter, terse, to the point. Euphemism is used to hide purpose. It shows the priggish insecurity of a newly arrived, up from the mud, middle class with their tedious effort to talk properly, not give themselves away.

"People know you by the words you use," Rush Limbaugh (antihero to P.C.ers) intones on a radio commercial. While he sells a vocabulary-enrichment program, the P.C. crowd struggles to reform, re-route, re-create the words we use, and with them the way we think about ourselves and our world.

They may or may not succeed politically. They may reorganize the lives of college boys with their humorless rigidity and fanatical authoritarianism, but they'll play hell de-slanging American speech or trashing its numerous artifactual equivalents.

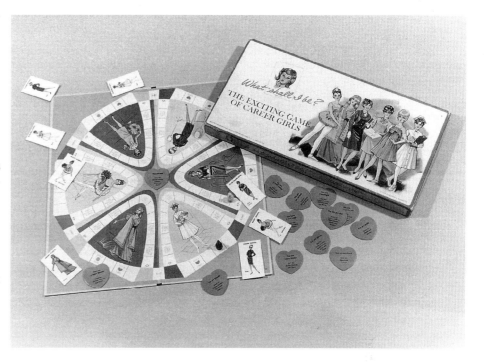

Advertising copy and toy makers conspire to reinforce gender stereotypes, which are intended to keep women in dependent roles, like motherhood, or in subordinate roles: nurse, not doctor; airline stewardess, not pilot; *fashion slave* (model); and so on and on.

BOARD GAME, "What Shall I Be?" Slechow & Righter Co., Bay Shore, NY. 1966. **$22.50.**

The Trickle Down Theory of Political Correctness, or How to Utilize a Dumbed-Down Version of P.C. to Deconstruct One's Own Workplace for Fun and Profit

While running the full P.C. word processing program requires an average IQ and that easy familiarity with big, clunky words that only college professors use, there are ways even *education-denied* and *IQ-deprived* malcontents can achieve substantially the same challenge to democratic social order. Look into the *cerebrally-challenged* speech codes and federal antidiscrimination laws. They are available from various P.C. outreach programs of most universities. In them you, too, may find evidence that you have been *victimized, harassed, discriminated against,* or *made uncomfortable* in the workplace. Somebody's got to pay. Find a P.C. lawyer. You may have taken the first step to a lawsuit-funded early retirement in a tropical clime.

On Pornography

Is the stuff in this book pornographic? Legally, no, in as much as it is openly sold in flea markets across the country. It is on the shelves and tables, not under the counter.

Some feminists' definitions of pornography, however, are pretty all-inclusive and the P.C. crowd loves to throw around epithets like "racist, sexist, homophobic, polluting," etc. We're really not scholars on this subject and are not interested in walking the edge of the First Amendment.

Most people, even radical feminists, distinguish between such categories as nudity, eroticism, explicit but mutually pleasurable sexual expression and the representation of violent rape. Undoubtedly there are P.C.ers who are even offended by Little Orphan Annie, but our intention, and for the most part, the intentions of the makers and consumers of this material is to make a gender joke or to titillate and occasionally, in a slangy but not illegal way, fire a salvo in the eternal war between the sexes.

"8 PAGE BIBLES," 1920s and '30s (also on opposite page). Not readily available in flea markets across the country, but you just might find one, if you ask, in trendier shops in major metropolitan areas. Although crudely drawn, sexually explicit parodies of comic strip characters, the depiction of women is often as willing, nay enthusiastic, participants.

Ads in the back of men's magazines often promise more than they deliver. U.S. postal regulations have largely through the years kept sexually explicit material out of the mails.

25

2. Classical Women

Everything about Venus de Milo, the most famous version of the Roman Goddess of Love, is politically incorrect, except that she is *handi-capable* (handicapped). One of the most reproduced objects of the ancients, the original marble statue was unearthed in 1820 on the island of Melos. Through the years numerous attempts were made to attach marble prostheses. Today she is exhibited at the Louvre in her "found" condition.

STATUE, 12" tall, gold painted plaster. 1950s. **$18**.

SALT & PEPPER SET, 4" high, plastic, in original box.
Marked: "#612 Venus Shakers © 1948 H. Fishlove & Co. Chicago." Spices pour from the breasts. There are politically correct aspects to this kitsch: along with the *melanin deprived* (white) salt shaker is a pepper shaker, a Venus *of color* (black). Both, you may note, just happen to be exceptionally *handi-capable,* as they are quadriplegic. **$25**.

The politically correct object to just about every aspect of the *Euro-American worldview* – including its origins in what we call the Classical World of ancient Greece and Rome. Political correctness can be seen to be something of a union between America's Puritanical tradition and radical post-Marxist theory. Neither group cares much for the ancient world and its various neo-Classical revivals. Political correctness rejects not only mainstream Christian tradition, it disapproves of such humanist icons as statues of naked humans, most of them *wimmin* (women), or the portrayal of unclothed or scantily clothed *wofems* (women) in oil paint or printer's ink.

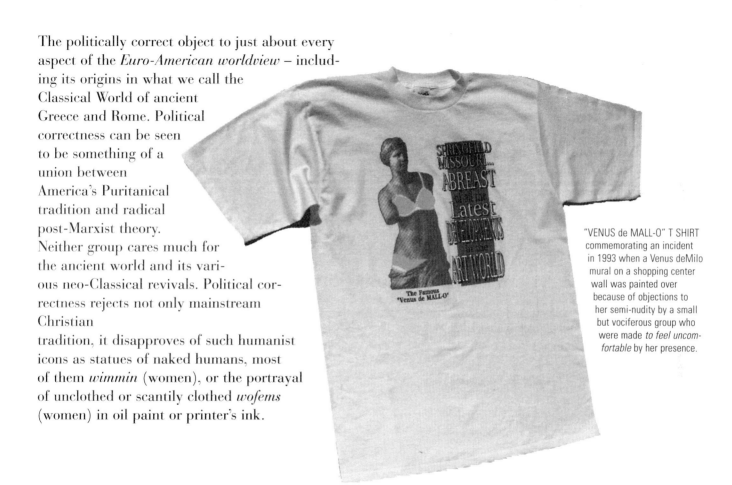

"VENUS de MALL-O" T SHIRT commemorating an incident in 1993 when a Venus deMilo mural on a shopping center wall was painted over because of objections to her semi-nudity by a small but vociferous group who were made *to feel uncomfortable* by her presence.

Puritans don't like sex (and there is an undeniable erotic element in even high European art) and radical leftists don't like the family (it challenges the authority of the state) which is often a consequence of the bonds of heterosexual love.

Upper-class interest in classicism ended abruptly with the Civil War and the deconstruction of the South, which was the bastion of American neo-classicism. There has continued, for various reasons, however, an unwavering devotion on the part of many ordinary people to the humanistic interest in near naked *wofems*. As we will see, this interest has continued to evolve. The semi-naked *fefem* (female) has stepped from the pedestal onto the calendar page. As blue-noses of old sought to remove Greek statues from drawing classes of the 19th century, today's P.C. wish to rip the girlie calendars and centerfolds from dormitory walls.

The ménage à trois between Psyche, Cupid and Venus is a soap opera saga. Our Victorian ancestors, high-minded and moralistic as they were, just couldn't get enough of plaster casts of semi-naked Greek goddesses in their parlors. They came in many sizes.

No. 756.—AMOR AND PSYCHE.

STATUE, 20" high, cast alabaster, 1888. Depending on condition today's value would be **$450-$850.**

BEER AD, Psyche for Schlitz, 18" x 24" lithographed cardboard, early 1900s. **$175.**

Latin is a dead language, and has been for a long time. Still, fragments of Roman mythology have floated around, inspiring delightful Victorian statuary, greeting cards, calendar art, etc. The Puritans have waged war for centuries against this salaciousness. The politically correct seek to finish off the glory that was Greece and the grandeur that was Rome.

MAILED ADVERTISING PIECE, 9" x 11" 1952. This pin-up version of a contemporary love goddess has borrowed Cupid's bow. **$3.50.**

FEBRUARY 1952

ELECTRICAL WIRE & CABLE DEPARTMENT
UNITED STATES RUBBER COMPANY

U.S. RUBBER
SERVING THROUGH SCIENCE

Hylas, *a heightism survivor,* is invited to a *gender sensitivity* training seminar at Mysia by two *vertically challenged* (tall) lesser divinities of nature (nymphs).

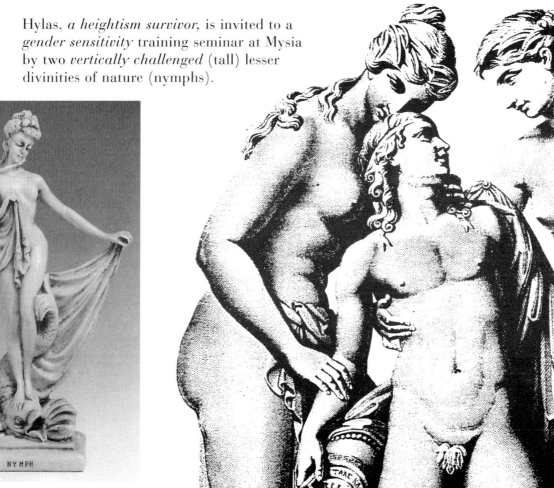

NYMPH STATUE, 9" tall, composition. Circa 1910. **$125.**

Mermaids

Mermaids are *aquatic seductrons* (sirens). The politically correct could accurately say they are *meremaids* because they symbolize *Wofem* (Woman) as the Spirit of Earth, as opposed to Man who is the Son of Heaven.

TV LAMP, 11" long, ceramic and plastic, 1950s. **$65.**

1. PAIR OF WALL DECORATIONS, 4" long, bisque. These little mermaids predate Disney's cartoon feature, but with their coy halters they display the same ignorance of their mythological origins. Mermaids are sirens, dangerous and sexy, who lure men to their deaths. 1950s. **$28/pair.**

2. PAIR OF WALL DECORATIONS, 9" long, painted chalk. not as well made as #1, but they show the come-hither look of the original *temptrons of the sea*. 1950s. **$14/pair.**

3. ADVERTISING PAPERWEIGHT, 5" tall, painted lead. Named "Tilghmaid" she advertised the Tilghman Packing Co. 1890s. **$85.**

4. NOVELTY, plastic and wire, in original box. "© 1954 H. Fishlove & Co. Chicago." **$25.**

Victorian reinterpretations of classical statuary were popular. One of the all-time favorites showed attractive young *womyn* (women) naked and often in bondage – more classical *sado-rituals of patriarchy*.

"Every young sculptor seems to think that he must give the world some specimen of indecorous womanhood, and call it Eve, Venus, a Nymph, or any name that may apologize for a lack of decent clothing."
– Nathaniel Hawthorne
The Marble Faun, 1860.

STATUE, 16" tall, bronze. Has paper label on bottom: "Armor Bronze, The Armor Bronze Corporation, New York City." Circa 1910. **$265.**

TABLE LAMP, 24" tall, wood, mother of pearl, several kinds of plastic and cloth. "Hi-Sense" and Chinese calligraphic characters. Neo-classical nudes on shade. Recent. **$30.**

SLAVE GIRL STATUE,
14" high, marble
composition. 1888.
$375.

La Source

An enduring piece of classical symbolism is the association of women with vessels bearing water (which is the symbol of women). To this day *wimyn* and their jugs are a favorite sexist image.

3. Adam and Eve

The politically correct would definitely have been *uncomfortable* living back in the Greek and Roman era. The dawn of Christianity did not usher in gender equality, for it has some distinctly politically incorrect aspects as well. Zeus was certainly an overbearing, bad-tempered patriarch, a mega-illiberal, but the God of the Hebrews and later the Christians put a planet together with plenty of *sexual discrimination*.

Consider the *text* of the Book of Genesis and the first case of *sexual harassment*. That Eve takes the rap is an indication of God's extreme prejudice and male domination. Eve tempting Adam to eat the forbidden apple, of course, means more than an unauthorized lunch break in Paradise. The business with the snake, *a differently honest* (lying) reptile, is a bad piece of animal rights p.r. – but we're saving that issue for our volume on ecology/animal rights.

The real corker, however, is the story of *male motherhood:* first, God the Father, the archetypal patriarch, creates the world, then he brings Eve forth from Adam's body. Both acts are a clear usurpation of *wimyn's* (women's) creative power. It's all been going downhill since then.

ADAM & EVE FIGURINES, 8" tall, low fire ceramic, Japan. Eve, by the way, hides an apple behind her back. Adam, a *male mother*, earliest victim of *vagina envy*, here is portrayed as the first *spouse abuser*. 1950s. **$37.50.**

STEIN, 10" tall w/lid, hand-painted home ceramic. 1960s. **$25.**

DIDN'T NOTICE

PREACHER—"Last night I dreamt I was in the garden of Eden."

MISS FLAPS—"Oh, my, how interesting. But tell me, did Eve appear as she generally is represented?"

PREACHER—"I—I—I—er, well to tell the truth I didn't notice."

* * * * *

THE REASON

Luke Warm claims that the reason why Adam and Eve didn't have an auto was because they lacked attire.

Slangy humor of the past is often inscrutable to us today.

CARTOONS from *Red Pepper* magazine, 1924 and 1925. $15/issue.

Eve, according to feminists, was "the dynamic, curious, anti-authoritative, active, courageous, powerful part of a couple of which the man is timid, anxious, and passive, doing what Eve orders. She was the first explorer in the world and didn't accept for-bidding (even by God) . . . our foremother." (Heide Reindl-Scheurering, 1984.)

ILLUSTRATION from
Art & Life magazine,
March 1927.

39

Early Girlies

Loopholes in censorship laws allowed "art" magazines containing renderings and photographs of seminude models and actresses in vaguely classical poses to be openly sold in the 1920s and 1930s.

$8-$12 each.

"When correctly viewed
Everything is lewd.
I could tell you things about Peter Pan
And the Wizard of Oz –
   there's a dirty old man."

– Tom Lehrer

4. Art and Naked Girls

Trying to sell the idea that *attire deprived* (naked), usually *melanin impoverished* (white) *lookist wimyn* (attractive females) are fit subjects for art is a time-honored business of the *exploitive Western patriarchy*. As mentioned before, political correctness took root so readily because of the Puritanical substrata of the United States which has *also* waged a 300-year war against all things that smacked of licentiousness or Classicism. As the Victorians presented their *attire deprived wimyn* as Greek goddesses, so nudes were labeled "Art" in the early twentieth century. Although the *politically correct* of yesteryear saw through this ruse and were definitely *made to feel uncomfortable* by these *exploitations of wimyn*, they didn't have the ear of p.c. college professors, administrators, or government bureaucrats at that time. Efforts to banish these mildly erotic pulps along with nudity in high art were generally unsuccessful.

Ads from the back of *Art and Life*, May, 1924. "The Body Beautiful, The Mind Intellectual, the Soul Intuitional." Strangely, some of this was for real.

Still, many of the ads bespeak a readership of *sexually focused, chronologically gifted individuals* (dirty old men).

1

No. 4412—Art View Scarf Pin. Horseshoe shape silver finish scarf pin set with whitestone brilliants. The center has an imported French view with assorted pictures of actresses and art subjects. A new and extremely fine selling number.
Per dozen..$1.75
Per gross $19.50

No. 4407—Platinoid Finish Art View Scarf Pin, cluster design, set with six fine whitestone brilliants. The center has an imported French view, the same as the horseshoe style pin.
Per dozen..$1.35
Per gross $16.00

2

ART VIEW RING

$13.50

Per gross

French Art View Rings

No. 4512—Made of metal, silver finish; set with one white stone brilliant at extreme top. The mounting contains "views" magnified by small powerful lens. Views include bathing girls, actresses, etc. A remarkable selling novelty item.
Per dozen.............$1.25
Per gross............$13.50

3

No. 4527—Novelty Art View Pencil. Regular hexagon lead pencil, with nickeled metal tip and rubber eraser, assorted colors. By looking through the opening underneath the metal tip you see photographic views of French art subjects, which are magnified by powerful lens.
Per dozen..................80¢
Per gross...............$9.50

1. ART VIEW SCARF PIN, 1929. **$35.**

2. ART VIEW RING, 1929. **$45.**

3. NOVELTY ART VIEW PENCIL, 1929. **$22.50.**

Stanhopes. Invented by an English lord, stanhopes were tiny lenses that magnified a tiny photographic image, frequently an "art view" of an *attire-deprived* (nude) *woman.* Often they were installed in jewelry, knife handles, etc. as a novelty.

REAL PHOTOS OF NUDES, 3³/₈" x 5³/₈".
"American Art Company" airbrushed
nudes in sylvan settings. In original
mailing box marked "pat. 1909."
There are 39 in all. **$200 ($5 each).**

ACCENT LAMP, 6¹/₄"
tall, pot metal with
bronze finish. 1920s.
$85.

45

1 *2* *3*

Art Nouveau was a design movement of the 1890s characterized by curvilinear form. What better place to get curves than from a woman's body? Later, the Art Deco style inherited the rage for nudes as decoration, resisting the severe Machine Age look of the 1920s and 1930s. Even in proper households in the first half of the century, nudes were acceptable adornment for compotes, vases, lamps and other middle-class household accouterments. Such objects today frequently bring two to three times the price of similar household items decorated with Scottie dogs or posies.

1. FLOWER FROG AND CANDLEHOLDER, 7" tall, glazed and bisque ceramic, Germany. **$65.**

2. VASE/URN, 8" tall, blue pottery. "Roseville USA 763-8." The line is called "Silhouette." 1952. Depending on condition: **$200-$350.**

3. VASE, 10" tall, green pottery, "Roseville Pottery 787-10." Silhouette, 1952. **$375.**

VASE, 14" tall, blue pottery, Van Briggle, Colorado Springs. Pattern is "Lady of the Lily." The company is still in business and a large selection of patterns are still being sold today. This piece was made in the 1970s. **$500.**

All three pieces are by Cambridge Glass Company, Cambridge, Ohio, which went out of business in the 1950s. From left to right:
GOBLET, 6" tall. This is a gold cup on a pink female stem. **$95/stem.**

BOWL, 9" tall, pink glass. "The Shell Bowl" came in several colors. 1930s. **$200-$225.**

COMPOTE, 8" high, ruby red glass bowl on clear female figure stem. 1940s. **$150.**

STATUE, 8" high, 12" long, ada clay green with brown.
"Fan Dancer" by Frankoma Pottery. 1940s. **$150.**

STATUE, 5" high. ada clay, green with brown accents.
"Dreamer Girl" by Frankoma Pottery. 1940s. It was originally
called "Weeping Lady." The name was changed when it
didn't sell. **$135.**

Opposite page:

OIL PAINTINGS ON CANVAS, 24"x20", 1950s. Signed on back "Ramon Van Gogh." True value undetermined. Acquired at Ventura Swap Meet for **$20./each.**

Ramon Van Gogh, a Hollywood set designer, nudie artist and drinking companion of Ed Wood, the B movie director, painted in a manner somewhat reminiscent of his better known great uncle, Vincent.

CARTOONS from *Hooey* magazine, 1932. $15./issue.

Scrupulous Attendant: "Will you kindly pull your skirt down, miss?"

51

5. Pinups

"Man should be trained for war and woman for the recreation of the warrior." — FRIEDRICH NIETZSCHE

During the war years of the 1940s, pictures of air-brushed, scantily clad, smiling, sexy women decorated the nose cones of bombers and were pinned up in tanks, toilets, and even tents. These pin-ups,

seen then as healthy, well-washed, athletic gals worth fighting for, are today politically correctly seen as the *fetishized recreational presence of women to reactivate the depleted forces of the warrior.*

Esquire magazine laid the legal and esthetic ground rules for the combination of girlie imagery and serious writing. The air-brushed dolls of *Esquire*, done by George Petty and Alberto Vargas (signed a. Varga) of the 1940s and early '50s would give way to photographed centerfolds in a magazine started by former *Esquire* employee Hugh Hefner. *Playboy* debuted in December 1953.

POSTCARD, 1940s. **$2.**

1. CIGARETTE HOLDER, 11″ long, painted plaster. A *temptron* so *lookist* that the *non-viable, non-human animal* (tiger rug) has come to life. 1940s. **$65.**

2. Esquire, January, 1955. 12 different calendar girls by George Petty are bound into the magazine. The complete calendar was available at newsstands everywhere. This issue, complete with all 12, **$22.50.**

3. WALL DECORATION, 13″ long, painted plaster. 1940s. **$85.**

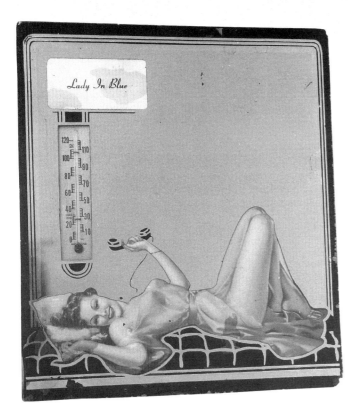

MIRROR/THERMOMETER, 8"x10," 1940s. **$65.**

VARGA CALENDAR, 1945.
Significant dates are circled.
On the 24th it says:"F.C. Davis
torpedoed, 77 out, 191 saved." **$195.**

STATE CLEANERS

Our Trade-Mark is Quality - Our Slogan is Service

1759 Silva Street
Honolulu, Hawaii

Phone 865355

CALENDAR, "State Cleaners,"
Honolulu, 1954. **$15.**

CALENDAR, "Trojan Market Co." Entitled "Ecstasy."
"Reproduced in tintogravure from the Original Pastel by
Zoe Mozert." The artist, a former model herself, painted in the
nude, often using herself as subject. "Mysticism, suspicion and
ethereal beauty are combined with eloquent composition
to make this a picture you'll always remember."
Brown & Bigelow, St. Paul, MN. 1954. **$45.**

WETMORE TOOL & ENGINEERING CO.

ENGINEERS — DESIGNERS — MANUFACTURERS

Special Carbide and Hi-Speed Cutting Tools

ANgelus 9-7266

5320 EAST WASHINGTON BLVD.   LOS ANGELES 22, CALIF.

TROJAN MARKET CO.

PRIME and CHOICE EASTERN BEEF

Hotel and Restaurant Purveyors
Wholesale Meats

922 W. Jefferson   Los Angeles 7, Calif.

PRospect 6469 - 3257

CALENDAR, "Wetmore Tool &
Engineering." 1960s. **$10.**

Incendiary sexist devices (girlie matchbooks) were produced by the hundreds of millions. Those advertising *misogynic habitats* (male-dominated business places) – bars, bowling alleys, gas stations, etc. – are especially likely to be graced by the near-nude female form.

1930s, catalog cut. **$1.**

1940s, Golden Years of Pin-up Art. **$3.**

1950s, still air-brushed art. **$2.**

1960s, uninspired photography. **$1.**

1 **2** **3** **4**

that Jantzen Girl is here again!

AD, drawn by Varga, 1941. **$5.**

Here she is, men ... the girl you love to look at ... on every beach, at every pool, wherever there's summer ... water ... fun ... wherever there's sunning or swimming to be done. She's every girl you know, every girl you want to know, made lovelier, more vivid, more exciting, by Jantzen's new "Lastex" swim suit fabrics, thrilling colors, foundation technique that really controls, a new Jantzen Beauty-lift Bra that really lifts. She's an exciting new interest coming into your life ... for her, look your best in trim athletic Jantzen trunks.

Mainliner ... 1941 Water-Velva sensation, as "Varga-ish" as it looks. 6.95
"The Surfer" ... Velva-Lure trunks, tailored the Jantzen athletic way. 3.95
Other Jantzens for Women 4.95 to 10.95   Men's Trunks 2.95 to 4.95

1 and *3*. RUBBER DOLL, 4" tall. When squeezed, she fetchingly utters a gleeful squeal. 1960s. **$12/each.**

2. GO-GO DANCER COCKTAIL SHAKER, 15" tall, rubber and plastic, battery operated. When turned on she vigorously shakes your drink. Plaque on front says: "When down at Freddie's, The Go-Go's the thing. You can't take her home, to feel like a king. We hope this gadget, puts your head in a whirl, namely your very own go-go girl." "©1969 Poynter Products Inc. Cincinnati, Ohio. Made in Japan." Mint –in original box– condition. **$45.**

4. CARNIVAL CHALK FIGURINE, 10" tall, painted chalk. 1940s. Has a distinct, "Goddess of the Early Nudist Beach" aura, with a convenient shot of green paint in the fig leaf zone. **$65.**

"Alberto Vargas came by his eye for beauty legitimately . . . his father was a famous portrait photographer in Peru. Alberto studied art in Zurich, Switzerland. At the age of 14 he toured all of Europe's famed art galleries viewing paintings and sculptures by the hour. His work attracted the attention of publishers everywhere . . . His big break came in 1919 when his full time was contracted for by Florenz Ziegfeld. Vargas 'glorified the American Girl on canvas' just as Ziegfeld 'glorified the American Girl on the stage.'

His biggest accolade came with the world-wide acclaim through the pages of *Esquire* magazine. His first 1940 Girl Calendar was an unprecedented success. After Pearl Harbor, the American G.I.'s took the 'Vargas Girls' to the four corners of the earth. Recognition for his efforts came from Peru wherein he received the medal and brevet of Knighthood in the Order Of The Sun. The American government accorded him a citation for meritorious service to the country.

This is your private collection of beautiful paintings from the master hand of Alberto Vargas – creator of beautiful women."

– Biography of the artist printed on the back of the Joker.

DECK OF PLAYING CARDS, 3½" x 2½". "Vargas," Creative Playing Card Co., Inc., St. Louis, 2, Missouri. 1940s. **$110.**

ADVERTISING CALENDAR NOTECARDS, 8" x 4¹/₂".
All by Elvgren. 1950s and early '60s. "Created by
Brown and Bigelow, St. Paul, Minn. USA."
$10/each.

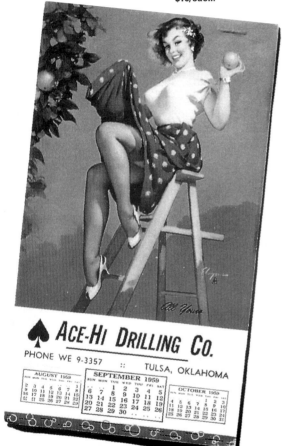

OIL PAINTING ON CANVAS, by Zoe Mozert, 1940s.
$3,500. Zoe Mozert not only painted the pictures,
she also posed for them. The voluptuous bod in
her works is often her own.

MUTOSCOPE CARDS, 5¼" x 3¼". "Made in USA,
B&B" (probably Brown and Bigelow). Some are
signed "Zoe Mozert" or "Earl Moran." Others are
unsigned. Average **$10/each.**

GOLF TEES, wood and pink plastic, "Made in the USA, Creative Products Mfg, Bethlehem, PA." 1960s. *Least best* (bad) ideas are persistent. **$10.**

What not, indeed? The female form, in whole or in part, has been molded, carved, cast and imprinted upon myriad materials through the ages to put in the hands of man a variety of useful objects.

GOLF TEES, colored plastic, The golf course is a sanctuary for the *male-dominated capitalist/rapist social order.* 1950s. **$10.**

PAIR OF WHATNOT SHELVES, 20" high,
jigsawn plywood, varnished. 1950s. **$50./pair.**

6. I am Woman, I am Whatnot Shelf

I am woman, I've been mugged

Many of these ceramic mugs were low-fired home ceramics and were crafted by women. Some were sold, some given as gifts. We've personally met many women who think they are funny.

SET OF 6 MUGS, 5" tall, ceramic. Female figure handle becomes progressively more *chemically inconvenienced.* Her green dress slips off and she finally dives in. 1950s. **$72/set.**

1. TORSO MUG, 6" tall, ceramic. Marked around the rim "Viva La Difference." A *differently sized, sun person* (woman of color). 1960s. **$15.**

2. LIBERTY BELL STEIN, 6", ceramic. combines sexism and nationalism for the *sobriety deprived.* Inscribed "To Flip from Nancy 12-25-79" While not particularly well made its multioffensive charm makes it worth **$20.**

3. BREAST MUG, 6" tall, ceramic. We've seen this classic in all sizes and ethnicities. This one just happens to represent the mammary of a person of the *mutant albino genetic recessive global minority.* They are still being made and distributed by novelty companies (described in their catalogs as: SEXY DRINKING MUG for the macho male. Drink from this genuine ceramic "boobie" mug.) A fair amount are out of home ceramic molds and are frequently gifts from the *domestic incarceration survivors* (wives) who made them for their *legalized rapists* (husbands). **$16.50.**

4. HEAD MUG, 4" tall, ceramic. Enigmatic home ceramic. Unusual in that it shows a detailed face. 1960s. **$10.**

5. MUG, 4" tall, ceramic. The breasts are wired to swing free with the tipping of the mug. Marked "Let Them Swing" and on the bottom "Patent T T." 1950s. **$28.**

6. TORSO MUG, 4" tall, ceramic. Small in size, it is laden with sexist metaphor. Full-figure handle on torso mug. On the back a molded set of legs above the inscription "The One I Love." 1950s. **$20.**

"And that Miss Jones is the way a torpedo works." "Great God – I said <u>kit</u> inspection."

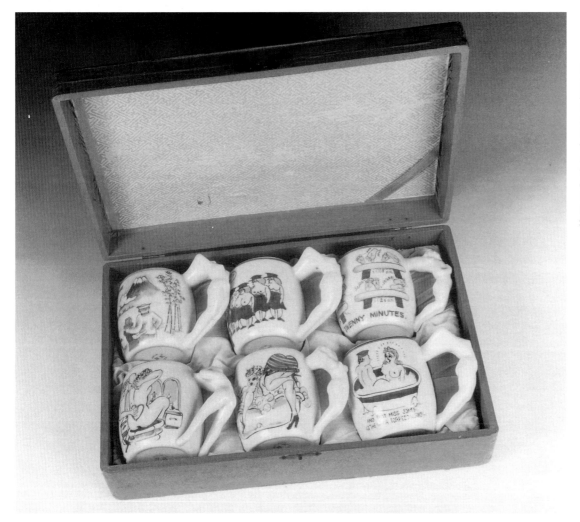

CASED SET OF 6 MUGS, 3" tall, hand painted porcelain. Marked "Made in Arita Y K" Japan. Made in the 1930s near Nagasaki for sale to English-speaking servicemen stationed in the Philippines and Hawaii. Torn hand-written note, dated Jan. 14, 1943, says: "Dad: I hope Mom and you like these, Have Mom make you some coffee in . . . Due back on ship." Mom may not have appreciated the humor. They've never been used. Rare. **$425/set.**

1. Lois James

2.

HAVE ONE "4" Corner Cafe

3. AL & Kitty's 4-Corners CAFE

Fine Food Where Hi-Way's 466 & 395 MEET

4.

I am woman, I am torso highball, vase or beer stein

"La Source" took on a highly diversified meaning in the postwar world. Sometimes sold through ads in the back of men's magazines, such incorrect wares were also readily available at souvenir stands and truck stops. The age-old concept of a woman's body as a functional container has continued to this very day, but with diminished exuberance and variety.

1. TORSO HIGHBALL, 5" tall, home ceramic. "Made by Virgia, 1953." **$16.50.**

2. GLASS, 7" tall, ceramic. Nude figure in bas relief outlined in gold. 1950s. **$12.50.**

3. SET OF 3 GLASSES, 6" (tallest), ceramic. They advertise "Al & Kitty's 4 Corner Cafe" by Pat Hogan. 1960s. **$35./set.**

4. TORSO GLASS, 6" tall, ceramic with rhinestone. Signed "Long." 1950s. **$20.**

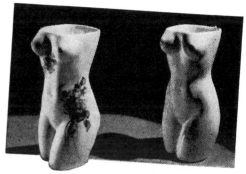

TORSO HIBALLS

Here's just the thing to shock a maiden aunt; but watch Uncle Foster's eyes pop when you serve him his night-cap in one of these ten ounce white ceramic torsos. What a full bodied drink that'll be! FLOWERED TORSOS are **$2.00 each.** BARE TORSOS are **$1.75 each.** (Postpaid, if your remittance accompanies your order.)

Esquire, August, 1949

Glasses with decals showing fetching lasses clothed and, on the other side, nude are not uncommon. Unfortunately, the decals are fragile and easily chipped. Decals were available separately if you wanted to decorate your own glasses. A 1950s ad from Johnson Smith and Company describes two of the many variations on a sexist theme. "MYSTIC Nudie Glasses – Liquid Brings Her to Life. One High Ball Makes Them Undress Before Your Eyes . . . With these 6 obliging little hostesses, the success of your party is 'in the bag.' Give your guests *a floor show* in every drink!"

SET OF 6 "NUDIE" GLASSES. 1950s. **$36/set.**

Iron Maidens

Women can be many useful objects: nutcracker, bootjack, ashtray and door stop. The fun puns and metaphors of the *phallocracy* are seemingly endless.

Page 74.

1. NUT CRACKER, 4" long, gold painted iron, "Adams' Streamlined Legs Nut Cracker." 1930s. **$37.50.**

2. NAUGHTY NELLIE BOOTJACK, 10" long, painted cast iron. Woman as lackey to facilitate removal of boots of the *privileged equestrian classes* (horsemen). Often reproduced, sometimes in aluminum. Original example, 1880s. **$85.**

3. ASHTRAY, 5" long, cast iron. A *vertically inconvenienced* (tall) *womyn* experiences *sexual harassment* of an undeniable form – see reverse side of ashtray on this page. An alternate *Story of O!* ("Oh!" is cast in the ashtray.) Also frequently reproduced. 1920s. Original examples: **$75.** Reproductions: **$15-$18.**

DOORSTOP LADY, 12" tall, polychromed cast iron, early 1900s. **$195.**

Sparkling Photo Handle Knife

No. 1750—Sparkling Handle Pocket Knife. Full brass lined; two blades made of hardened and tempered steel heavy beveled nickel silver bolsters and rivets. Fancy handles with nicely colored photographs of beautiful art subjects on both sides. Length closed, 3½ inches. One dozen in box, no less sold.

Per dozen... **$4.00**

No. 1751—Sparkling Handle Pocket Knife. Full brass lined, two blades made of tempered steel, heavy beveled nickel silver bolsters. Fancy iridescent handles with nicely colored photographs of beautiful art subjects on both sides. Length closed, 3¼ inches.

Per dozen............................... **$3.85**

No. 1752—Sparkling Photo Handle Knife. Transparent iridescent celluloid handle; assorted colors, gold, silver, emerald, ruby. Photographs of stage and bathing beauties on both sides of handle; brass lined; nickle silver bolsters; 2 blades made of fine tempered steel. Length closed, 3 inches.

Per dozen **$3.75**

Popular Priced Photo Handle Knife

No. 1798—American Made Photo Handle Knife. Two steel blades, nicely polished, brass lined, with assorted art subjects. Length when closed, 3 inches. This is the biggest value ever offered.

Per doz. **$2.40**

ART KNIVES, 1929. **$35-$45.**

The Cutting Edge of Fetishism

Photo View Knife

No. 1701—Art View Knives. Each knife contains picture of dancing girl or bathing beauty which can be seen through miniature magnifying glass contained in one of the ends of each knife, has two blades, brass lined, assorted stag and celluloid colored handles. Length of knife, when closed, 3 in.

Per dozen........................ **$3.75**

PHOTO VIEW KNIFE. A stanhope with photo of dancing girl or bathing beauty. 1929. **$45.**

MARILYN MONROE POCKET KNIFE. **$35.**

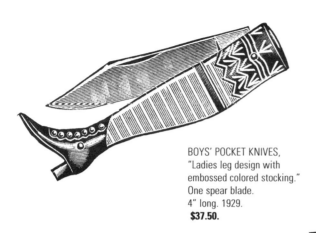

BOYS' POCKET KNIVES,
"Ladies leg design with
embossed colored stocking."
One spear blade.
4" long. 1929.
$37.50.

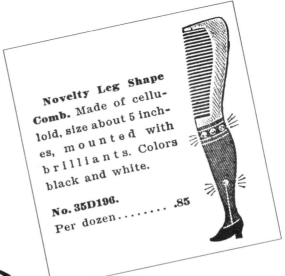

Novelty Leg Shape Comb. Made of celluloid, size about 5 inches, mounted with brilliants. Colors black and white.

No. 35D196.
Per dozen........ .85

1. LETTER OPENER, 8" long, cast aluminum. An advertising piece from "Central Pattern and Foundry Co., Chicago." 1930s. **$50.**

2. LETTER OPENER, 8" long, pink plastic. Imprinted on reverse: "Out on a limb? Place your ad here. Leg Letter Opener Drawing Guide." 1950s. **$20.**

3. LETTER OPENER, 8" long, amber plastic. Advertising piece designed by Elvgren, a famous calendar artist of the 1940s and 1950s. Anything by Elvgren is highly collectible. 1950s. **$35.**

4. BALLPOINT PEN, 5" long, flesh colored plastic. The use of ladies' limbs is common in small personal objects used by men. The practice goes back well into the 19th century. 1960s. **$12.**

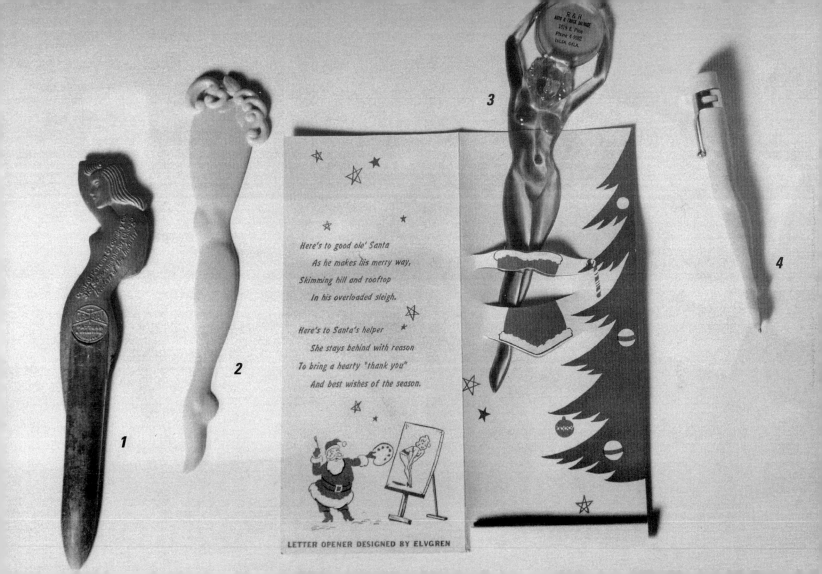

1

2

3

R & H
AUTO & TRUCK SALVAGE
1615 E. Pine
Phone 4-9882
TULSA OKLA.

4

Here's to good ole' Santa
    As he makes his merry way,
Skimming hill and rooftop
    In his overloaded sleigh.

Here's to Santa's helper
    She stays behind with reason
To bring a hearty "thank you"
    And best wishes of the season.

LETTER OPENER DESIGNED BY ELVGREN

BIRTHDAY CARD, ©1948, "A Novo Laugh."
Slip the white strip of paper behind the cellophane
and she slips out of her evening dress into her
underwear. **$8.**

Temptrons of Transportation

HOOD ORNAMENT,
9" long, chrome plated
metal with amber
plastic wings,
mounted on marble.
1940s. **$45.**

BUG DEFLECTOR,
5" tall, plastic.
"Santay Queen Bug
Deflector For Safer
Driving Clear Vision,"
Santay Corporation,
Chicago, Illinois.
A version with red
plastic screen is seen
on the right.
1950s. **$40.**

In days of yore *marauding Western imperialist plunderers* in sailing ships parted the waves with bare-breasted carved wood female figureheads. In the more recent past *mobile environmentally degrading pollution delivery systems* (automobiles) driven by the descendents of these *global rapists/capitalists* mounted bare-breasted chromium goddesses on the hoods of their Detroit rolling stock. Some of these femmes of the open road served a useful purpose as well as being beautiful: Queen Bug Deflector.

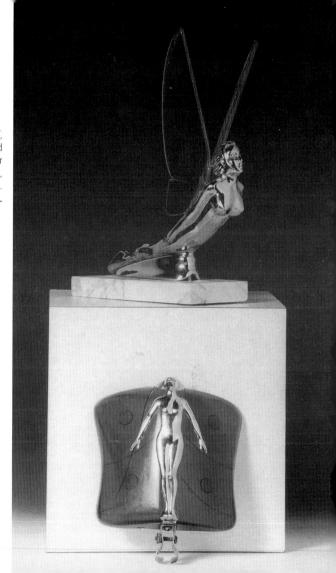

Scatalogical Sexist Silliness

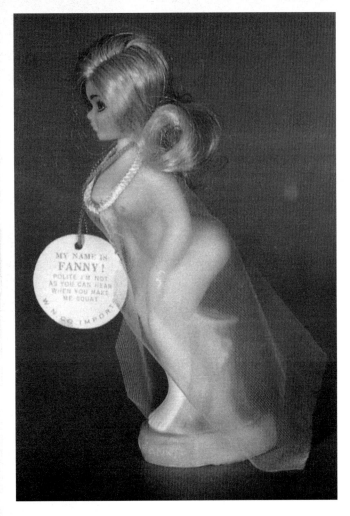

OUTHOUSE SALT & PEPPER SET, 3" tall, Japan. 1950s. **$15.**

FARTING FANNY, 6" tall, painted rubber. "W N CO Imports." When you push her down she makes a rude noise. 1950s. **$17.50.**

Puzzling Women

Men have often claimed that women are hard puzzles to solve. Women often feel they are seen as nothing but pieces.

PLAYBOY PLAYMATE PUZZLE, "Complete Playboy Centerfold Miss December Cynthia Myers ©1967." **$35.**

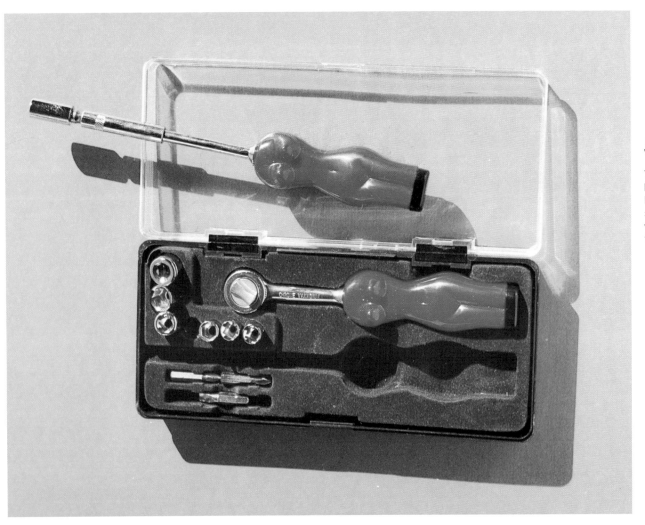

Socket to me baby!

TOOL SET, 9" x 4" (case size).
Plastic and chrome-vanadium.
Red plastic handles on the
screwdriver and socket
wrench combo. Tool time
from Taiwan. 1970s. **$35.**

Women are so handy to have around the house.

Miss I've-Got-My-Love-To-Keep-Me-Warm

WATER BOTTLE, 23" tall, painted rubber.
Poynter Products, Inc. Cincinnati, OH.
1967. Her *bell-person* hat is actually the
screw-on cap which is often missing. **$75.**
Flea market dealers may call her either
Jayne Mansfield or Marilyn Monroe.
We think she's just a generalized
blond bombshell.

TITTY PILLOW, 14" long, pink and purple plush. A *fetishized* object for the *maturation deprived* (immature) male. 1970s. **$15.**

Differential framing (the habit of the *phallocracy* to portray men's faces and *wimyn's* bodies) has as its ultimate expression the well-known fixation of American men on female breasts. As you will see, not all this fetishism is dysfunctional. Many of the breast-fixated novelties are useful objects. Further recognition of male preoccupation with mammaries is indicated by the number of slang expressions for them: bags, bazongas, bazooms, boobies, boobs, cans, coconuts, globes, headlights, hooters, knockers, lungs, mangoes, melons, pair, tatas, and tits to name a few.

1. PLAYBOY PACIFIER, ©1968, Franco-American Novelty Co. New York City. Flesh color and pink rubber. This has been in continuous production for years. A current box gag is called "A Pacifier for Lover, complete with retaining neck strap." The new ones sell for about $6. retail. Older ones go for **$17.50.**

2. HAPPINESS TOOTH BRUSH, rubber and plastic. Also in continuous production: *least bad* (good) ideas never *become nonviable* (die). **$4.50.**

3. TOOTHBRUSH AND RAZOR SET, plastic, "Made in France, Fox Trot Paris." One hundred years ago French postcards were synonymous with "filthy pictures." This smartly designed set shows that the French are still celebrating "la difference." 1970s. **$8.**

Playboy Pacifier

7. Double Trouble

HAPPINESS TOOTH BRUSH

EXCELLENT FOR HEALTHY GUM MASSAGE

FOAM

1

2

3

COASTERS, painted rubber, 1950s. **$24.**

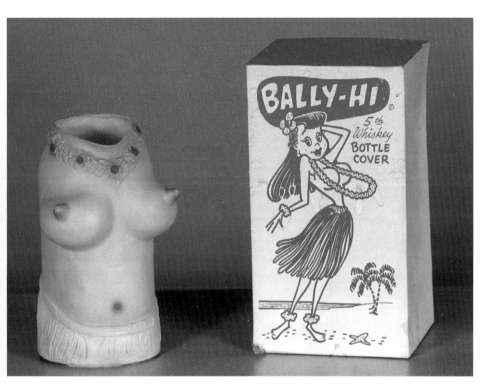

BOTTLE COVER, painted rubber, 1950s. Instructions recommend that you coat the inside with talcum powder to help ease your favorite bottle into this mammary masterpiece. **$28.**

PLASTIC CUP, "BUSTY," 5" tall, 1950s. It rattles when you shake it. **$17.50.**

KOMIC KARDS, 9″ long. Made in Japan. Truly tacky titillation. 1950s. **$3.**

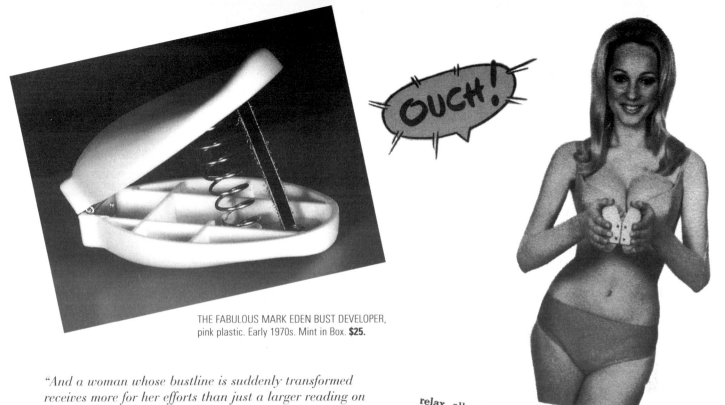

THE FABULOUS MARK EDEN BUST DEVELOPER,
pink plastic. Early 1970s. Mint in Box. **$25.**

"And a woman whose bustline is suddenly transformed receives more for her efforts than just a larger reading on the tape measure. She is subtly transformed as a woman. There is an incomparable difference in the entire feminine line, shape, and grace of her whole figure. Her very presence takes on a new and subtle glow of womanliness, of sex appeal and, yes, of glamour that is undeniable and unmistakable."

relax, allowing the exerciser to open, then immediately repeat by closing again, relaxing, allowing to open again, close again, etc., at a steady, even pace. Repeat for 20 repetitions; that is, you will close and open the exerciser 20 times. On the last repetition, that is, on the 20th time you close it, do not let it open immediately but hold it closed for as long as it takes you to count to 8 . . . about 6 to 8 seconds. This marvelous movement will affect the entire bustline.

Payton's Law: Political incorrectness is perversely proportional to the number of slang synonyms or the amount of garden variety metaphors used to describe a person, thing or activity.

Pulp periodicals of the '50s are especially rich in double trouble humor.

P.C. fems have not completely repressed bawdy booby humor and metaphor as these T-shirts recently acquired at the I-44 Swap Meet attest. "Can't keep in 'em," grinned the vendor. A lot of gals buy them for their guys.

"You and your damn sudden stops!"

"Two jugs . . . er, two coffees please."

Also: gazongas, baby pillows, poonts, bra busters, hooters, boobs, headlights, knockers, jugs, titties, bee-bites, tatas, bazooms, snorbs, love-bubbles, big brown eyes, balloons, cans, pair, tremblers, twin loveliness, milk shop, etc.

Wine, women, and a deck of naked girl playing cards in a smoke-filled room constitute a perfect evening's entertainment for many *income-challenged, socially inconvenienced* (poor lowlife) males. In truth, *sobriety deprivation* (drunkenness) and *nicotine dependency* (smoking) in the company of *easily accessed sex care providers* (easy women) are general tendencies of **all** socio-economic classes of men. *Domestic incarceration survivors* (wives), as well as radical feminists, find such behavior incorrect.

1. LIQUOR DECANTER, 11" high, ceramic. What man wouldn't feel like a king with this whiter than white temptron sitting saucily atop the "Old Man's Private Stock?" Has a crown for a stopper. 1960s. **$30.**

2. LIQUOR DECANTER, ceramic enhanced with rhinestones. Her head is the stopper. This easy woman on an easy chair appears to be *a person presenting herself as a commodity allotment within a business doctrine* (prostitute). Japan, 1950s. **$27.50.**

3. LIQUOR DECANTER, 10" high, paper label says "G. Nov. Co. Japan." It is widely recognized that alcohol is used by men to make women *chemically inconvenienced* (drunk), facilitating *date rape* (seduction). "Candy is dandy, but liquor is quicker." And in this case it pours from her breasts. 1950s. **$30.**

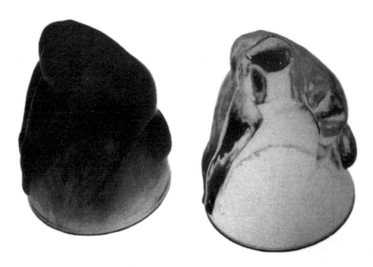

BOTTOMS UP CUPS, 3" high. Early 20th century. Depending on color of glass and whether or not they have their own fitted glass coaster, the price can range from **$65.** to **$175.**

8. Boozie Floozies and Smoking Sexpots

1 "HANDS OFF!" "OLD MANS" PRIVATE STOCK

2

3 LAY OFF This is the Old Mans PRIVATE STUFF

I am woman, I am the spice of life

Salty wenches all. These ceramic novelty salt and pepper shakers are sure to shake up the politically correct. Perfect to spice up a pair of sunny-side-up, cholesterol-rich *non-human-animal products stolen from poultry* (eggs). Such a breakfast, however, may tend to make you *horizontally challenged* (fat). The enduring popularity of these novelties has kept some of them in production. Similar versions are available at select sexist retail locations.

SALT & PEPPER SET. 7" long, ceramic with rhinestone inserts. Paper label says: "A Quality Product, Japan." A real jewel of a set of shakers, this could be the high point of anyone's kitsch collection. 1950s. A steal at $18.50 but worth **$37.50**.

Opposite page, clockwise from center.

SALAD SET. 11" long, ceramic, Japan. The mother of all shakers: the head dispenses salt, the breasts oil and vinegar, the legs, pepper. 1950s. **$65.**

SALT & PEPPER SET. 6" long, likely home ceramic. Has been rendered dysfunctional by gluing the breasts to the body. Glazed black, it shows that sexual puns can be equal opportunity offenses. Age uncertain. **$12.**

SALT & PEPPER SET. 6" long, ceramic. This one is unusual in that she looks you right in the eye. The addition of hand painted detail would seem to date this in the 1950s. **$27.50.**

SALT & PEPPER SET. 4" long, ceramic, Japan. Not happy in her work, she covers her face with her arms. 1960s. **$15.**

SALT & PEPPER SET. 5" long, ceramic. Has that Venus of Willendorf look. 1970s. **$12.**

SALT & PEPPER SET. 6" long, ceramic. Triangular paper label says "G. Nov. Co. Japan." 1950s. **$17.50.**

SALAD SET. 7" long, ceramic, Japan. One leg is salt, one pepper, and the breasts hold oil and vinegar. 1960s. **$35.**

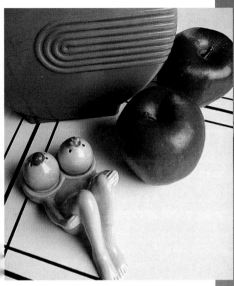

Let's lay it all out on the table: Sex and food are the obsessions of all men. For once the feminists may have gotten it right.

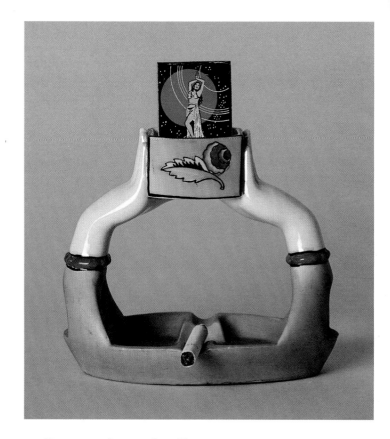

Since our foremother Eve gave into temptation,
women have been associated with leading men
into various vices – smoking, drinking, gambling,
and debauchery – all lavishly portrayed in the
high and low art of the West.

Women are not just beautiful, they make handy-dandy useful objects: holding up light bulbs, gracing liquor jars, ornamenting vases, opening bottles or letters, even cracking nuts.

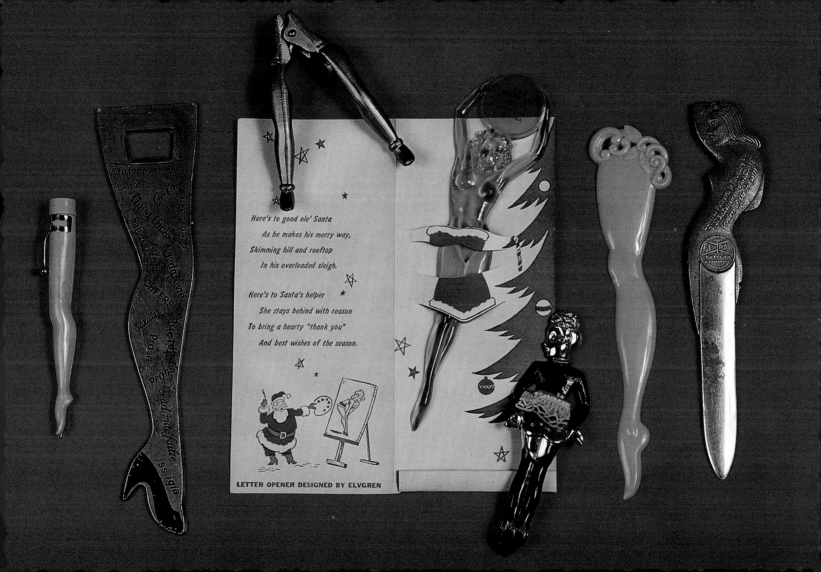

Here's to good ole' Santa
As he makes his merry way,
Skimming hill and rooftop
In his overloaded sleigh.

Here's to Santa's helper
She stays behind with reason
To bring a hearty "thank you"
And best wishes of the season.

LETTER OPENER DESIGNED BY ELVGREN

While the majority of women's images in flea markets are of compliant, seductive, appealing babes like hula girls, a sharp-eyed collector can still find the occasional pirate girl, cowgirl, witch or WAC that can be seen as politically *correct*.

A World O' Hurt

Wimmin (women) are not the only victims of the *melanin-deprived, testosterone-poisoned, genocidal Eurocentric patriarchy* (white male world order). The flea markets of America are loaded with an artifactual record of the shameful mistreatment of African-Americans, Native Americans, nature and all that is cute, endangered or exploited within it. We are at work on future volumes on these subjects. Men, the source of all this grief, will have a *larger than standard size* (fat) P.I.C. tome of their very own.

Probably there are other offended groups out in the psychobabbling/deconstructed/left outback deserving similar recognition. Please let us know of such groups or artifacts. Or for membership information, contact P.I.C.A. (Politically Incorrect Collectibles Association), 3020 S. National, #340, Springfield, MO 65804.

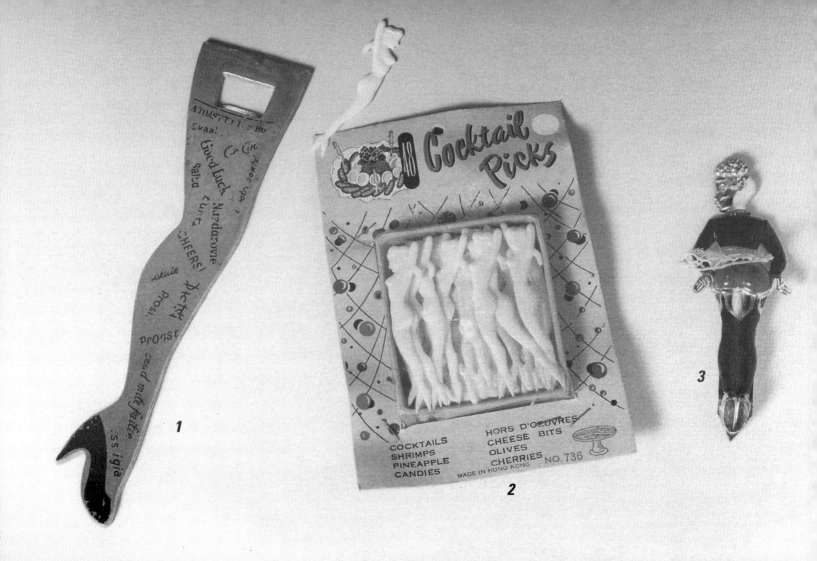

1

2

48 Cocktail Picks

COCKTAILS
SHRIMPS
PINEAPPLE
CANDIES

HORS D'OEUVRES
CHEESE BITS
OLIVES
CHERRIES NO. 736

MADE IN HONG KONG

3

CORKSCREW AND BOTTLE OPENER,
10" long, painted aluminum
"Barmaid" who has a *cerebrally
challenged* (stupid) expression.
"Made in Italy." 1940s. **$85.**

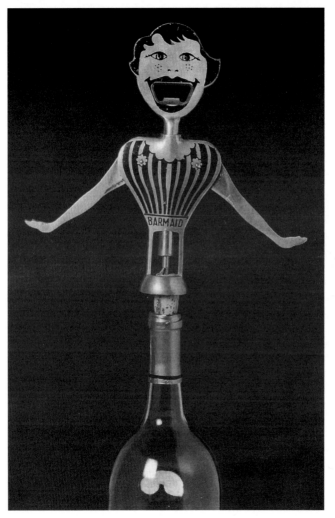

1. BOTTLE OPENER, 10" long, *non-ferrous fetishistic tool*
(aluminum bottle opener) for the *sobriety-deprived malt
beverage consumer* (beer drinker). 1940s. **$40.**

2. COCKTAIL PICKS, *pigment-impoverished non-organic
material* (white plastic) representations of *attire-deprived
wimyn* (nude women). 48 to the pack. Recent. **$5.**

3. BOTTLE OPENER, 5" long, plated and painted
with cloth apron. "Fifi, the Church Key," an *oppressed,
economically exploited, live-in survivor* (maid church key)
made *indefinitely idle* (unemployed) by the pop top can. **$12.**

APRON, cotton. A *waitron* offers a choice of beer, whiskey, or foam rubber breasts. Even more sexist than "Coffee, Tea, or Me?" 1950s. **$35.**

POCKET FLASK, nickel plated metal. *Wimyn* have been associated with leading men astray since Eve. 1930s. Because of poor condition its value is **$25.**

POSTCARD, Mirror-Krome,
San Francisco, 1950s. **$2.**

PENTHOUSE PETS "SWIZZLE STRIPPERS,"
©1976, Poynter Products, Inc. Cincinnati, OH
$24.50.

Ad from N. Shure Co., Chicago, World's Largest Novelty House, 1931. Today this reclining woman ashtray would be worth **$22.50.**

Ad from Johnson Smith and Company, Detroit. The catalog is dated 1950, but the illustration could be much earlier. Many of the items in these novelty catalogs date from much earlier—even as much as 50 years or more. Mermaid ashtray. Today's value **$25.**

1. CIGARETTE LIGHTER, 5" tall, plastic and white metal. Marked "Silent Flame Table Lighter, Parker of London, Made in U.S.A." A slurred Nouveau goddess atop an inelegant Art Deco base. Indifferent design is somewhat balanced by the fact that it is an early battery-operated labor-saving device for the convenience of the capitalistic *patriarchial hierarchy* (males). 1930s. **$35.**
2. CIGARETTE LIGHTER, 2" tall, metal. Marked "Supreme Japan." Babes in bathing suits on all sides. 1950s. **$20.**
3. CIGARETTE LIGHTER, 3" tall, soft plastic. "Made in Taiwan." This contemporary lighter comes in a multitude of color combinations. A superior version exists and was prominently featured in the remake of *Cape Fear* starring Robert DeNiro. That version features nipples that light up when struck. New. **$1.75.**
4. ASHTRAY, 4" long, ceramic. A professionally designed and nicely made, high-fired ceramic. Probably sold in the back of men's magazines. 1960s. **$22.50.**

I am ashtray, cigarette lighter, matchbook, multi-purpose temptron of the tobacco industry. Doubly and sometimes triply assaultive are these appropriations of women's image. Where there's smoke, there's fire in the eyes of the politically correct.

"*Nature in the Raw is seldom MILD*"

THE PILLAGE OF PARIS

"Nature in the Raw"—after the great French artist Lumais ... inspired by the savage fierceness of untamed Norseman in the ruthless capture of Paris—845 A.D.

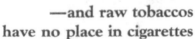

—and raw tobaccos have no place in cigarettes

They are *not* present in Luckies ... the *mildest* cigarette you ever smoked

WE buy the finest, the very finest tobaccos in all the world—but that does not explain why folks everywhere regard Lucky Strike as the mildest cigarette. The fact is, we never overlook the truth that "Nature in the Raw is Seldom Mild"—so these fine tobaccos, after proper aging and mellowing, are then given the benefit of that Lucky Strike purifying process, described by the words—"It's toasted". That's why folks in every city, town and hamlet say that Luckies are such mild cigarettes.

"It's toasted"
That package of mild Luckies

"If a man write a better book, preach a better sermon, or make a better mouse-trap than his neighbor, tho he build his house in the woods, the world will make a beaten path to his door."—RALPH WALDO EMERSON.
Does not this explain the world-wide acceptance and approval of Lucky Strike?

Rape or seduction, victim or temptress. The extremes of feminine appeal have been used to stimulate tobacco sales for decades.

Ad in *True Detective,* November, 1932. **$12.**

Ad from *Ladies Home Journal,* June, 1950. **$8.**

Scientific tests prove Lucky Strike milder than any other principal brand!

These scientific tests, confirmed by independent consulting laboratory, prove Lucky Strike mildest of 6 major brands tested!

MARLENE DIETRICH says:
"I smoke a smooth cigarette—Lucky Strike!"

Let your own taste and throat be the judge! For the rich taste of fine tobacco—for smoothness and mildness ...
THERE'S NEVER A ROUGH PUFF IN A LUCKY!

L.S./M.F.T.—Lucky Strike Means Fine Tobacco
So round, so firm, so fully packed—so free and easy on the draw

111

Beach Babe Ashtrays

ASHTRAY, 3" x 6", ceramic. "Watch Your Butt, Hawaii." Anything Hawaiian is hot. 1970s. **$18.**

ASHTRAY, 7" long, stoneware. Fully detailed on back. An example of blatant *faceism* (the practice of showing men's faces and women's bodies). 1960s. **$16.50.**

ASHTRAY, 8" diameter, ceramic. Hand painted accents. A Florida temptron is menaced by a *reptile-American* (alligator). 1960s. **$12.50.**

ASHTRAY, 5" square, ceramic. Marked "Peek-A-Boos ©1961 F Wilkinson 5111-W." Observed through a keyhole, the unclothed female on the phone says, "No, I haven't anything on for tonight, but I will have." **$12.**

"NO I HAVEN'T ANYTHING ON FOR TONIGHT, BUT I WILL HAVE "

ASHTRAY, 7" square, ceramic. Eyeing her martini, the *sobriety-deprived* (drunk) woman claims, "I just drink to be sociable." 1950s. **$16.50.**

ASHTRAY, 4" diameter, ceramic. Marked "Shenango China, New Castle, PA. 1940s. **$15.**

Come On Baby, Light My Fire

CIGARETTE LIGHTER, 2½" tall, stainless steel. Has a different nude in bas relief on each side. 1950s. **$42.**

CIGARETTE LIGHTER AND FLAT CASE. Engraved nude on one side. "Fuzi." **$69.50.**

TABLE CIGARETTE LIGHTER, 3" tall, bronze, Germany. 1930s. **$69.50.**

All of these are home ceramics or small commercial workshops utilizing purchased molds and low-fire kilns. Often given as gifts, any insult to female dignity is purely unintentional. They follow the long *white-male-heterosexual-dominated Western sexist tradition* of decorative objects which view the unclothed or semiclothed female form as a thing of ultimate beauty.

ASHTRAY, 10" long, ceramic. "T I E Ceramics." Abundant inn many color combinations. **$16.50.**

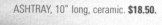

ASHTRAY, 10" long, ceramic. **$18.50.**

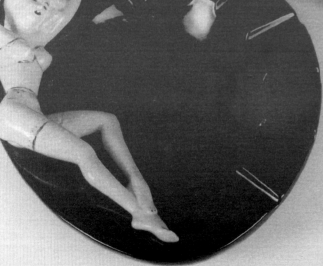

ASHTRAY, 11" long, ceramic. Marked "Ceramics by Yettieve." Made from a Fresno, California, mold dated 1955. We've seen this in a nude version. One could paint the bathing suit on or let her bask on your coffee table in the all-together. **$22.**

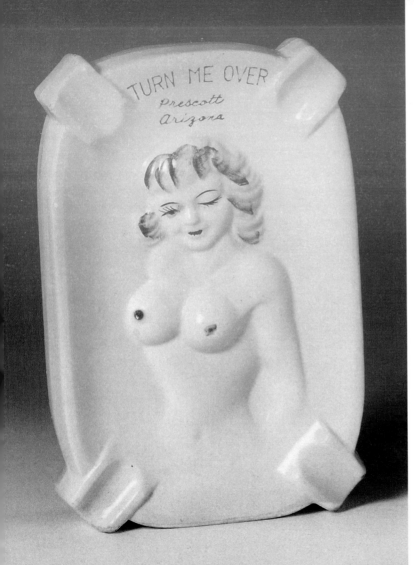

Not so innocent, these raunchy ashtrays clearly spring from the *misogynic* mind of *phallocentric* man. They could be seen as *sex-based insults uniting, in a consumer article, degradation, intimidation* and mediocre ceramic craft. Not to mention the socially incorrect act of smoking.

1. ASHTRAY, 5" tall, ceramic with rhinestone nipples. "Original ArtMark Made in Japan." A *horizontally challenged* (fat) *ashperson* who is masochistically inscribed "For Your Hot Ashes." 1950s. **$18.50.**

2. ASHTRAY, 5" long, ceramic. Paper label says "Japan." Inscribed "For cooling Butts and Ashes." 1950s **$22.50.**

3. SOUVENIR OF PRESCOTT, ARIZONA – DOUBLE SIDED ASHTRAY, 6" long, with rhinestone nipples. "Japan." The front (seen on the left) says "Turn Me Over." The back says "For Your Hot Butts and Ashes." 1950s. **$25.**

For Your Hot Butts and Ashes

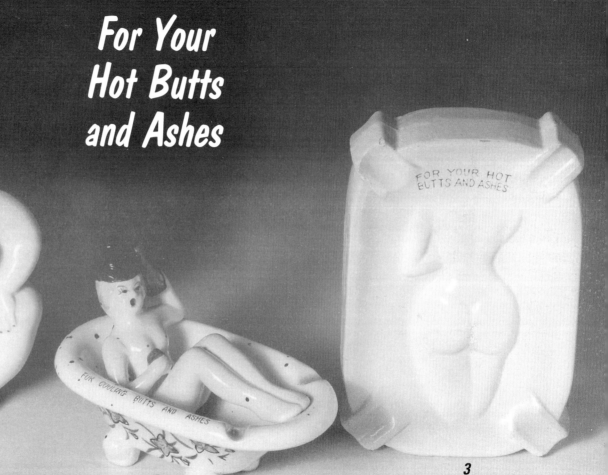

1

2

3

Metaphors Galore

SAY WHEN? **RIGHT AFTER THIS DRINK!**

POSTCARD, 1960s. **$2.**

APPLE "HONEY" and FRESHNESS go together like He and She

...ine tobacco to make a fine cigarette, but it takes something else, too! It takes *freshness!*

Apple "Honey"—the nectar of luscious apples—helps keep in the natural freshness of Old Gold's fine tobacco, to which "something new has been added"—imported Latakia tobacco for richer flavor.

Try Old Golds and see why they've won a million new friends!

Buy more War Bonds than you think you can afford!

Old Gold
CIGARETTES
THE TREASURE OF THEM ALL

OLD GOLD

ASHTRAY, 7" long, ceramic.
1950s. **$32.**

"A WOMAN IS ONLY A
WOMAN, BUT A GOOD
CIGAR IS A SMOKE"

POSTCARD, 1911. **$3.**

CIGARETTE LIGHTER, 2¹/₄" tall, Supreme, Korea. 1960s.
$12.50.

"Flap - A - Lite" Cigarette Lighter.

Artistically modeled head. Made of cast metal, bronze plated finish. Height 7 inches. Completely wired with socket, cord and plug, and automatic switch. Lights automatically when lifted. Packed each in box.

No. 29C69. Per dozen...... 10.50
Each .... .90

CIGARETTE LIGHTER, from N. Shure Novelty House catalogue, 1931.
Today's value **$125.**

MATCHBOOKS, 1940s. **$1-$3.**

CARTOON FROM *RED PEPPER*
MAGAZINE, October, 1924.
$15/issue.

PLAYING CARDS, "Fifty-Two Art Studies," © Novelties Mfg & Sales Corp. St. Louis. "Introducing for the approval of the discriminating artist and connoisseur of art, fifty-two separate and distinct art studies. These are an example of modern photography at its finest and should prove invaluable in discussion, etc." says the Extra Joker card. True artist's models don't wear make-up, lipstick or paint their nails. These, dear readers, are girlies. 1950s. **$25.**

PLAYING CARDS
designed by Elvgren.
1940s. **$35.**

BRIDGE SET, Fox Co.,
Philadelphia. **$22.50.**

PLAYING CARDS,
© B & B, U.S.A.
Also designed by
Elvgren. **$35.**

PLAYING CARDS "Royal Flushes
with 54 glorious nudes," Made in
Hong Kong, 1970s. **$12.50.**

MINIATURE
PLAYING CARDS,
"54 different
pin-up designs."
Printed in Taiwan.
1 3/4" x 1 1/2" **$15.**

MEN'S PULP MAGAZINES.
The staple features of these magazines were bondage, harems, Nazis, bikers, nymphomaniacs, and large-breasted women (occasionally in the same article). The ads in the back addressed the needs of their blue collar GI generation readers: hernia care, inflatable love dolls, mail order brides, correspondence schools and sea monkeys ("Own a bowlful of happiness.")
1950s pulps **$3.**
1960s pulps **$2.**
1970s pulps **$1.**

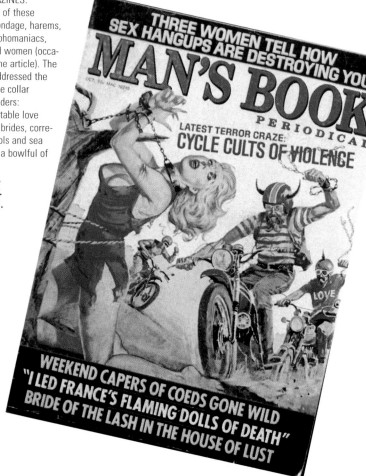

124

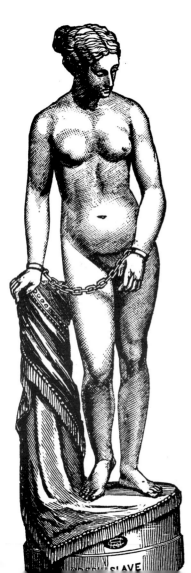

9. Victims

In the wacky world of the culturally over-sensitive, *wimyn* are, of course, considered the ultimate victims of the *Western white male phallocracy.* And, indeed, as this chapter shows, there is undeniably a sadistic/masochistic principle at work in male-female relationships. However, the radical feminist analogizing of sexism with racism is nonsense. That is a metaphor that stretches the credulity of the average woman, who is both better informed about the primitive state of evolution of the male mind than the radical p.c.'ers and vastly more adroit at manipulating men to their more civilized purposes.

STATUE, 40" tall, cast alabaster, reproduction of "Greek Slave" by Hiram Powers. This oft-reproduced sculpture of a nude in chains was to the Victoria gentleman a naughty-but-nice combo of pseudo-classicism and mild erotica. When first exhibited at the U.S. Centennial Exposition in Philadelphia, it drew crowds of viewers who waited for hours to see it. This example is from 1888. **$1,800.**

DIME DETECTIVE,
December 1948.
$6.50.

SPEED MYSTERY,
March, 1944. **$6.**

THE SHADOW,
October, 1941.
$8.

RANCH ROMANCES, August, 1959.
"His voice wasn't nearly as authoritative as he intended it
as he said, 'And I'm the boss, savvy?'
She smiled and rubbed her cheek against his, 'Yes, master.'"
From "A Desert Chase," a story in this issue.
$4.50.

Cult magazines from the 1930s, 1940s, and 1950s confirm the well-known truism that women do *indeed* need the protection of strong men or they face the unspeakable terrors of *blood-identified non-human flying mammals* (vampire bats) or *self-released clients of the penal system* with *difficult-to-meet needs* (escaped psychopathic killers).

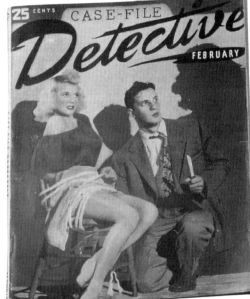

CASE-FILE DETECTIVE,
February, 1946. **$7.50.**

THE MASTER DETECTIVE,
January, 1930. **$12.50.**

THE MASTER DETECTIVE,
October, 1930. **$12.50.**

POSTCARD, 1940s. **$2.**

128

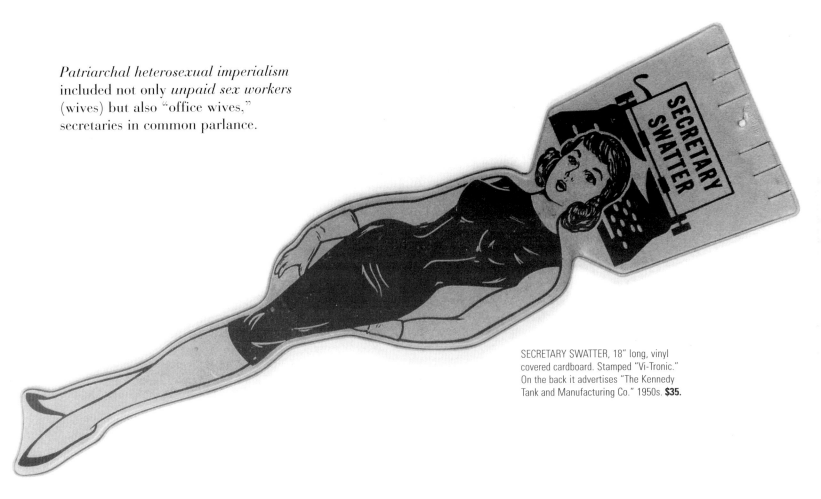

Patriarchal heterosexual imperialism included not only *unpaid sex workers* (wives) but also "office wives," secretaries in common parlance.

SECRETARY SWATTER, 18" long, vinyl covered cardboard. Stamped "Vi-Tronic." On the back it advertises "The Kennedy Tank and Manufacturing Co." 1950s. **$35.**

GARTER INSPECTOR BADGE, nickel plated metal. 1950. **$12.**

WOLFING LICENSE, nickel plated metal. "Here is your permit to go WOLFING. For those of you who do not understand this sort of slang, we will clarify the meaning of this term. It means an ABLE GABLE (a neat bundle of he-man), A GOOD TIME CHARLIE (a guy who is working the numbers racket – dating plenty of gals). FEMALE ROBBER (date stealer), NECK-HAPPY (a spooner); and in other words A BIG TIME OPERATOR who looks at anything. Get in the big time and start going after the gals – get your WOLFING LICENSE." In 1950 it cost 15 cents, postpaid. Today one in good condition would fetch **$15.** (And if worn in a p.c. workplace might get you 15 years.)

So's Your Old Man

Blondes Prefered

Let Me Tickle You

I Never Walk Back

My Weakness Wine Women & Song

Kiss Me I Wont Bite

I Know MY Onions

Naughty But Nice

BLONDES PREFERED

SO'S YOUR OLD MAN

In the darkness before the dawn of feminism, one could proudly display one's ignorant chauvinism by buying celluloid buttons with snappy sayings in packs of 100 for 85 cents. Good deals llike this are not likely to return – not only due to inflation, but also due to the overall severe deflation of *inappropriately directed laughter*. Today's price **$2.50 each.**

As this illustration from a 1929 novelty catalog demonstrates, the male will to power and domination over females begins early in life and is openly encouraged by such toys.

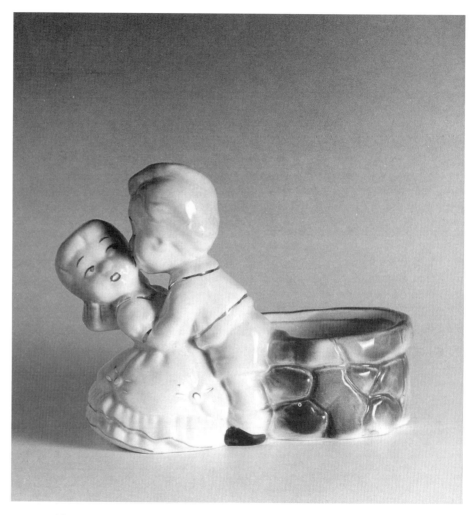

PLANTER, 5 ¹/₂" tall, ceramic. A *date rape* planter: he plants an unwanted kiss on her unwilling cheek. 1950s. **$15.**

133

Abusive humor goes way back. This is an ad from the N. Shure Co., Chicago, "The World's Largest Novelty House," catalog, 1931. These *patriarchal playthings* are catalogued under "Blowouts, Slappers, and Party Frolics."

WIFE BEATER

WHANG

The Wife Beater. Made of extra tough paper, corrugated and folded with riveted handle. Red, white and blue. When you slap with this it produces a loud, smacking noise; 13½ in. long. 1 dozen in bundle.

No. 26N9. Per gross 3.60
Per dozen .... .33

Abuse

Extreme examples of *patriarchal heterosexual imperialism* were thought hilarious in pre-feminist America.

A CHANCE TO LEARN

MR. BELOW (angrily) :—"For heaven's sakes, what are you doing up there?"

MR. ABOVE—"Beating up my wife."

MR. BELOW (excitedly) :—"Can I come up an see how it's done?"

C-C-CRACK

Wife Beater

No. 5705—Carnival Slapper or Wife Beater. Made of extra heavy paper in red, white and blue colors. The paper is corrugated and folded into a riveted handle. By slapping anyone on the back with this, it produces a loud, smacking noise. Length, 17 inches. One dozen in bundle.

Per dozen........25¢
Per gross....$2.50

Awareness of domestic violence and testosterone-driven brutish behavior did not just recently spring full-blown from the minds of the politically correct. Flea market finds from the turn-of-the-century on reveal ironically a more diverse and candid attitude than the industrial-strength, state-imposed morality and nagging-Nanny, authoritarian preaching of P.C.

"*Let's keep out of it – he probably has a good reason.*"

1950s cartoon

1911 book on the ills of strong drink

His memory blighted, and his senses parylized, the drunkard returns too late. What comfort can such a beast be, whose touch is polluting, and whose harrowing remorse is mocked by agonizing recollections?

WIFE BEATERS PERMIT

LONG LIVE THE KING

THIS CERTIFICATE IS AWARDED TO _____ TO FRAME AND HANG (IN THE RUMPUS ROOM). IT WILL CONSTANTLY REMIND YOU OF YOUR AUTHORITY TO FLY THE COOP ANYTIME YOU BECOME FED-UP WITH YOUR PECKIN CHICKEN.

NEXT TIME IT BECOMES NECESSARY FOR YOU TO TAKE YOUR PROPER PLACE AS HEAD OF THE HOUSE, TRY CROWNING YOUR QUEEN, THEN, PARADE WITH THE STAR SPANKING BANNER (SCARS AND STRIPES), AND YOU WILL BE QUALIFIED TO JOIN THE "MENS REVOLUTION", TO REIGN FOREVER AS "KING OF THE WHIPPER SNAPPERS".

BY _____

WIFE BEATERS PERMIT, 8 x 10" fake parchment.. 1957. **$5.**

I'd like to be a caveman
And drag girls to my lair;
To dress them up in nifty skins
Of tiger and of bear!
And every night I'd beat them up
And kiss their tears away;
I'll say I'd like to do this—but
I'm ninety-three today!

1924 humor magazine

SET OF DECORATED TUMBLERS, 6″ tall, 1950s. **$35/set.**
Others in the set, by the way, show the cavewoman bashing back.
Women's revenge and even aggression are more commonly depicted
in older material (before the victimology bureaucracy began editing
popular culture) than in contemporary headlines (see Chapter 14).

CHINA HEADED DOLL, 18" long, kid body. 1909. **$450.**

DAGUERREOTYPE OF GIRL WITH DOLL, one-eighth plate, circa 1850. **$250.**

10. Oh, You Beautiful Doll

The androgynous ideals of political correctness find dolls objectionable in a number of ways. They are gender-typing tools. From baby dolls to Barbie dolls they encourage *prewymin* (girls) to think of themselves as mothers, flirts, sex objects. They reinforce the gender stereotypes of *traditional patrimony*. The word "doll" is also a *lookist* pejorative. "She's a living doll."

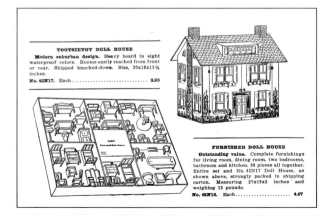

TOOTSIETOY DOLL HOUSE

Modern suburban design. Heavy board in eight waterproof colors. Rooms easily reached from front or rear. Shipped knocked-down. Size, 20x16x11½ inches.

No. 42N17. Each................................ 2.25

FURNISHED DOLL HOUSE

Outstanding value. Complete furnishings for living room, dining room, two bedrooms, bathroom and kitchen. 39 pieces all together. Entire set and No. 42N17 Doll House, as shown above, strongly packed in shipping carton. Measuring 27x18x3 inches and weighing 13 pounds.

No. 42N18. Each................... 4.67

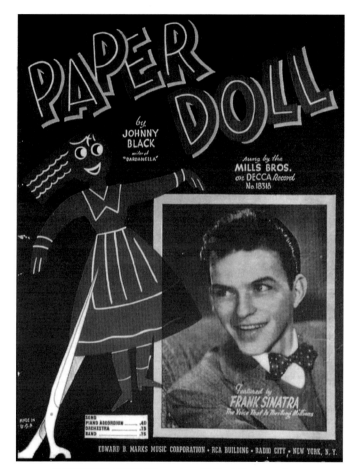

SHEET MUSIC, ©1915. This version with Frank Sinatra on the cover is 1943. "I'd rather have a paper doll to call my own than a fickle-minded real live girl." **$5.**

Barbie and Ken travel the Friend Ship in Stewardess and Pilot Outfits

Each outfit

$2⁹⁷ dolls not included

1 Barbie's up and away in this stylish outfit ensemble. Includes two blouses, a groovy vest, slacks, belt, a skirt and shoes. Shipping wt. 5 oz.
49 C 31021 ....$2.97

2 Ken's really in command in this high-flyin' outfit. Includes shirt, tie, jacket, slacks, shoes, cap and flight log. Shipping wt. 5 oz.
49 C 31022 ....$2.97

Barbie is the ultimate American doll. Introduced at the Toy Fair, New York, in 1959 by Mattel, she is believed to have been inspired by the German "Bild Lilli" doll, which was based on a newspaper cartoon in the early 1950s. Unlike most dolls, Barbie had the ideal feminine figure – long legs and arms, small waist, high round breasts, and long neck. Every girl who had one soon learned the skills of consumerism. There are literally thousands of outfits, accessories, vehicles, houses, etc., for her and her fashion-conscious friends. She's highly collectible and some of the early ones bring thousands of dollars.

SEARS CATALOG, 1962. Through most of her career Barbie was an airline stewardess, teacher, ballerina, or secretary. But in the '80s her feminist consciousness was raised and she became an astronaut in a hot pink space suit.

1. BARBIE BAG, 12 x 10 ½," blue vinyl, 1962. "Ponytail by Mattel." "As is" **$15.**

2. PONYTAIL BARBIE DOLL, 11" tall, 1960s. **$135.**

3. BARBIE TRUNK, 13 x 10 ½," black vinyl, "Ponytail by Mattel." 1961. **$70.**

1

2

3

142

No. 164—Whoopee Doll.
Has the appearance of a life
size baby. Nicely painted
and trimmed with crepe paper bonnet, cloth diaper and
large 4-inch Safety Pin.
Height, 16 inches. 16 to
barrel. (No less sold.)

Each .... **85¢**

Today's value **$25.**

Most cultures have had little surrogate human figures that children played with. The mass-market dolls of America accumulate in flea markets and junk shops awaiting adoption by collectors. Mass-produced in enormous quantities, few achieve the commercial success of Barbie.

In case you've been asleep for the last 40 years or you're an alien visitng Spaceship Earth for the first time, be advised that you should not address a *wofem* as "doll." The gift of a doll to a *pre-wofem* (girl) is also considered insensitive and ill-advised as it imparts gender stereotyping.

KOMIC KARD, 9" long, made in Japan. **$3.**

THE THREE KINDS OF WOMEN—

MRS.   MISS   MISSED

The capacity to sustain abuse and the appetite for it (love) and *legal sanction for rape* (marriage) no longer go together like a *non-human equine animal* (horse) and carriage. There is abundant cynicism and skepticism about love and marriage in the *male-stream* (mainstream) as well as in the p.c. world. Still, men and women continue to engage in this dangerous game. The artifactual record reflects these misgivings.

POSTCARD, circa 1910. **$5.**

As these advertisements from catalogs and magazines from the 1920s to the '60s illustrate, dolls are mostly female and have served a wide variety of purposes.

"This doll is for older kids; when you put her to bed, she closes her eyes and says "Daddy"

11. Love and Marriage

TRUE ROMANCES, August 1924. **$10.**

DREAM WORLD Into the Land of LOVE and ROMANCE, January, 1927. **$15.**

TRUE ROMANCES, July, 1924. **$10.**

POSTCARD, E.C. Kropp Co., Milwaukee, 1940s. **$2-$5.**

In Western society compulsory heterosexuality is learned early. *The passive pleasers of any and every man* (women) have been coercively programmed to submit to the political and economic structure of the patriarchy. Dating intiates the subjugation.

Illustration from *As You Sow*, a 1911 cautionary tract on drinking. Then as now there were vehicles for *rendering the woman submissive, dependent and obliged* (sexual bridges) like candy and flowers.

CARTOONS FROM *HOOEY*
MAGAZINE, May, 1932.
Today's *potential date rapist*
should be advised that "yes"
means "no," "maybe" means
"no," and "no" means "no."

High blood pleasure.

DECORATIVE OBJECT, 4" tall, painted
metal. Revere MFG., USA, 1950s. **$10.**

149

POSTCARDS, 1940s. **$2-$5.**

For radical feminists the compulsory heterosexuality of the West *renders invisible the lesbian possibility.* That some women claim to like and/or appreciate the opposite sex only shows how deeply they have *internalized their oppression.*

CARTOON, *RED PEPPER* MAGAZINE, February, 1925, from the short story "Moonlight Spasms."
"Charles – please! Won't you? – " She leaned perilously near, her lips pursed in an inviting curve of red moist kissableness and stretched her arms open to him.

The wedding ceremony:
a *matriarchal totalitarian event* in which the bride is the central figure because the real change in status is hers . . . [Through this ritual] a woman is transformed from an economically dependent child to an economically dependent adult.
— *Marcia Seligson, 1973*

WEDDING CAKE COUPLES. The older ones in bisque can bring from $25 to $125. Illustrated are recent ones in plastic and bisque. **$2.50 to $25.**

BLUE BOOK,
September, 1914.
$15.

Mother in the Kitchen

With a prayer on her lips and a desire to serve *the patriarchal unit intended to enslave women and children* (family) these ceramic kitchen aids are distinctly p.i.c. The tallest is 6½". 1950s. Japan.

TOOTHPICK HOLDER (has original toothpicks) **$18.50.**

NAPKIN HOLDER (with the especially desirable and uncommon blond hair.) **$22.50.**

NAPKIN HOLDER. **$18.**

SALT AND PEPPER SET. **$18/pair.**

Housework: Tidy Torture

The *State of Servitude* is imposed on women by the inescapable, endless demands of "female" occupations and preoccupations: cooking, cleaning, childcare. It begins early and old ads like this show the method of imprinting *pre-wim-min* (little girls) and *legalized rape candidates* (brides).

Little Sister Sweeping Set. Consists of broom, floor mop, long handle dust pan and carpet sweeper. Length of broom, 32 inches. Mop 27 inches, dust pan 23 inches, sweeper 24 inches. Packed each set in a box.

No. 38N130.
Per dozen.... **12.00** | Each... **1.10**

MOTHER IN THE KITCHEN SPOON HOLDER, **$18.50.**
NAPKIN HOLDER, 9" tall, ceramic 1950s. **$15.**
VASE. 8" tall, ceramic, 1950s. **$17.50.**

DISHTOWELS, silk screened cotton, 1950s. They celebrate the joys of vacuums, household appliances and other labor saving devices – the message being "love your servitude." In unused condition these fetch **$12-$18.**

For the p.c., *unpaid, non-unionized, menial labor* (housework) performed by *domestic incarceration survivors* (housewives) is the eventual outcome of love, romance, and boyfriends.

SIFTER, 5 ¼" tall, enamelled metal. "Androck Hand-i-Sift pat. no. 2,607,491 3 Screen," 1952. **$35.**

Stranded in Suburbia...

When suburban fathers go off to work—
as suburban fathers must—their absence is
felt in more ways than one.

The "Stranded in Suburbia" syndrome.
This ad from *Fortune*, May, 1956, sug-
gests a solution for *an unpaid sex worker*
(wife)'s imprisonment: a Ford Fairlane.
Most would not escape in two-toned
Detroit chariots but would stay on to
become an *incubator, hotel, home and
hatchery for human souls* (pregnant).
It's an updated, suburban version of
BPBP (Barefoot, Pregnant and Behind
the Plow) of earlier, rural America.

KNOCKED UP NODDER, 6 ½"
tall. Paper label says "Original
Dee Bee Co Imports Hand
painted Japan." 1950s. **$15.**

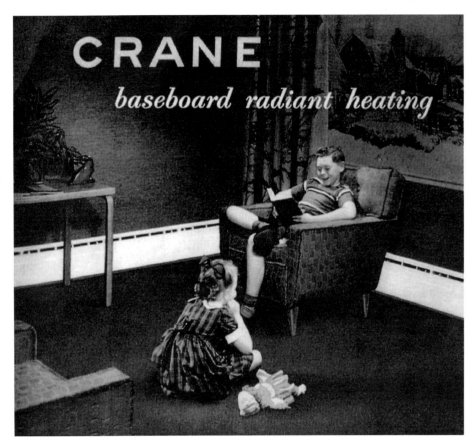

Magazines from the 1940s and '50s are especially rich in objectionable portraits of heterosexual couples, *the basic unit of the political structure of male supremacy.* In the heterosexual couple and the family unit, love and sex are used to obscure the reality of oppression and prevent women from identifying with each other in order to revolt.

Mass-circulation magazines from the 1940s and '50s are appreciating fairly rapidly. They can be had for **$3** to **$15** per issue, unless they have a Rockwell or sports cover. The gorgeous old *Esquires* with Vargas or Petty pinup art command higher prices, too.

> "Housebroken: condition of women taught/trained to 'live' in the Domesticated State: state of being tractable, polite, tamed, subdued, heart-broken/spirit-broken."
> – *Mary Daly, 1994*

Now with ORLON, Holiday Colors in Shape-Keeping, Sudsable Jersey!

This holiday season, celebrate at home — or go visiting — looking your loveliest in a new kind of festive jersey. Choose from deep winter reds, greens, golds, blues. No one will guess — but it's as washable as your own two hands. The secret? Du Pont "Orlon". And that's not all. "Orlon" makes news in other ways . . . in its touch that's whisper-soft . . . in the way it keeps its figure, whether sitting through a movie or off on a trip. And you'll wear this jersey oftener, since washing's so easy. Just suds, rinse, hang dripping wet. With light hand pats, it almost presses itself. Dries trim and soft, ready for fun.

Whether in dresses for you, suits for dad or son, or curtains for your home, "Orlon" acrylic fiber makes for easy-going *truly modern* living. Ask for it when shopping.

"Orlon" is Du Pont's trade-mark for its acrylic fiber

Couples...and their discontents

INDIGENOUS ALASKAN COUPLE FIGURINE, 6" tall, low-fired ceramic, signed "M.M." Recent. **$10.** Especially offensive because native peoples are assumed to be free of the sexist conventions of white males.

"HAPPY ANNIVERSARY" COUPLE, 4" tall, hard plastic. "Berries, 1971, Made in Hong Kong." **$7.50.**

"KEHONI" (THE KISS) FIGURINE, 6" tall. Signed "Frank Schirman, 1973" on side. Paper label on back declares "Made in Hawaii BEAUTIES WITH BLACK CORAL from the deep tropical seas of the Hawaiian Islands. Designs by Frank Schirman." **$8.50.**

TO ERR is HUMAN..

POSTCARD, "Greetings from Sheridan, Arkansas." 1950s. **$1-$3.**

SALT AND PEPPER SHAKERS, 4³/₄" tall, ceramic, Japan, 1950s. **$18.** These show the two sides of marriage.

A female *abundantly supplied with adipose tissue* has been an oft-pranked theme in the *dominant culture* (mainstream). Men *of substance* are not persecuted to the same degree as are corpulent women.

FATOPHOBIC POSTCARDS. 1940s. **$2.50.**

ALTER EGO FIGURINES or YOUR OTHER SELF. Paper label says: "or if we could only say what our conscience dictates..."
1. PAIR OF FIGURINES, 5" tall, ceramic. "He says I'm the model type . . . Yea, Model T." Marked on bottom, "Alter Ego ©1959." Japan. Silver label: "Vona Original Shafford, Japan." **$24.95/pair.**

2. PAIR OF FIGURINES, 5" tall, ceramic. "I love to eat like there's no tomorrow . . . The rate you are going there won't be." "Alter Ego ©1959" Japan. Silver label: "Vona Original by Shafford, Japan." **$24.95/pair.**

12. Fat and Funny

HE SAYS I'M THE MODEL T...

YEA...MODEL T...

1

I LOVE TO EAT LIKE THERE'S NO TOMORROW

THE RATE YOU ARE GOING THERE WONT BE...

2

IT'S THE SAME OLD MOON

BUT–HOW IT HAS CHANGED !

LINEN POSTCARD, 1930s **$1.**

Women with an alternative body image

SET OF 3 WALL PLAQUES, 12" high, painted aluminum. Marked "© Sexton 1968 USA." *Sizeism survivors* (fat) bowling team. **$22.50/set.**

The way the female strays from the ideal physical form has been a perennial source of American humor, especially in jokes, cartoons and comic postcards.

1. FIGURINE, 5" tall, ceramic, Japan. A multifaceted victim. Obviously she is a *weightism survivor* (fat). The anguished expression, disheveled dress and bottle tucked under one arm could also indicate a *sobriety deprived* (alcoholic), *involuntarily undomiciled* (homeless) person. 1960s. **$18.**

2. COIN BANK, 5" tall, painted plaster. 1950s. **$25.**

3. STATUE, 14" tall, painted, low fired ceramic. A *horizontally challenged* (fat) woman of near mythic proportions. 1970s. **$16.50.**

4. CANDY CONTAINER, 16" tall, painted particle board with lucite and pipe stem cleaner. Anthropomorphized *non human animal with an eating disorder.* The breast cavities are filled with candy, the head and neck are the stopper. Sleep on it, neo-Freudians. Crude and recent, doubtlessly inspired by Miss Piggy, but when is the last time you saw another? Difficult to put a value on. We paid a buck at a garage sale.

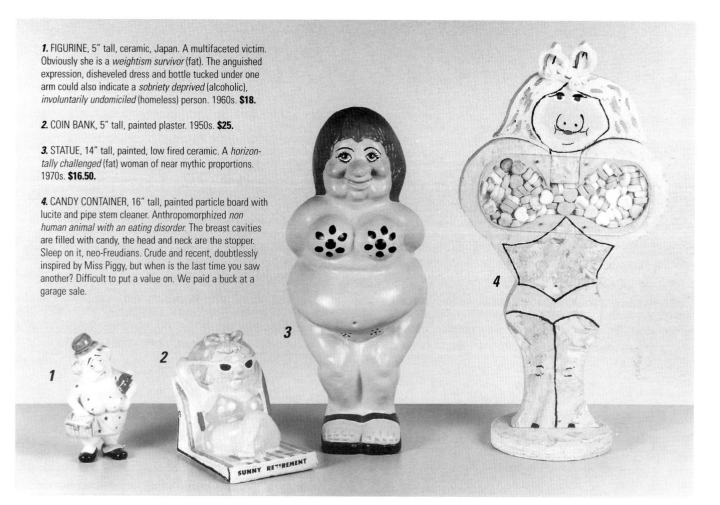

SUNNY RETIREMENT

FULL MOON
Hosiery

Just imagine what happens to the woman who is hose-conscious! No woman with her toes wiggling around loose in her shoes can put her mind on her work.

Happy feet are very important to a woman. If she's worrying about her socks, chances are she will go out and dance with some gigolo just to forget. And then her husband walks in and socks her. Next thing we know she has wound up in Reno all run down. Would that be nice? Well, it all depends.

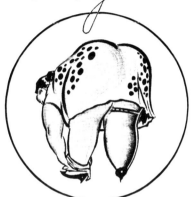

*"The hose that comes up
to your expectations"*

These four cartoons from 1932 issues of *Hooey* and *Ballyhoo* magazines (value **$8-$12 per issue**) exploit the image of *wimmin who just happen to be differently sized.*

"I'm putting everything in the hands of my attorneys."

Size-ist humor in this case is especially offensive because it is directed at activist feminists.

"We pedestrians must do our bit."

"I regret to see such a mere handful here to-night."

Another double whammy *oppressed-within-the-oppressed status* (victim) is the Native American *womyn*. Indians are classic victims of the *eurocentric/cultural deprivation framework* (systematic denial of the right to exist of any culture but a European-based one). The treatment of *copper women* (Native American women) by chiefs and bucks has been the subject of mini-ha-has.

TWO BUCKS ON THE LINE

AD FOR SPRING MAID SHEETS. Even by the antediluvian standards of the 1940s and 1950s, the ad copy of Elliot White Springs, a World War I fighter pilot and owner of Springs Cotton Mill of Lancaster, SC, was judged offensively sexist. *Male-stream* (mainstream) publications frequently refused to run them. 1950. **$3.**

13. Multicultural Babes

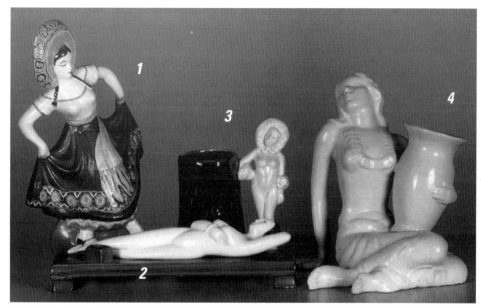

The center slice of *Turtle Island* (the U.S.A.) is, of course, culturally diverse, as the multiculti bevy of beauties, cuties and Mammies in this chapter attests.

POSTCARD, a "Laff Gram" from Amarillo. 1950s. **$2.**

1. MEXICAN FIGURINE, 11" tall, home ceramic polychromed. Decorative objects with a Mexican theme are abundant in the U.S. They were especially popular fromt he 1930s through the 1950s, as a result of Roosevelt's Good Neighbor Policy. Recent. **$12.50.**

2. ORIENTAL DOCTOR'S FIGURINE, 10" long. Synthetic ivory on wood base. There are old figurines like this made of real ivory. The apocryphal explanation for them was that Chinese women were so shy that rather than disrobe and submit to examination, they would point to the figurine to show what hurt. Recent. **$35.**

3. NAN-NOOKIE OF THE NORTH ESKIMO GIRL MUG, 6" tall, green ceramic mug, beige handle. Marked on bottom: "Riddell ©1952." **$17.50.**

4. HAWAIIAN GIRL WITH JUG VASE, 8" tall, ceramic. Probably 1950s. **$35.**

Pop culture portrayals of Mexican *womyn* emphasize traditionally dressed peasant women either bringing water or dancing.

The pop culture portrait of the Mexican male inevitably shows him sleeping or strumming the guitar. That must be why she works so hard, fetching or being fetching.

Her-spanic Honeys

1. BOOKENDS, 6" tall, painted plaster. Unusual imagery as señor seems to be helping with a domestic chore. 1930s. **$25.**

2. LAMP, 11 ½" tall, painted plaster. 1930s. **$45.**

3. DECORATIVE OBJECT, 9" tall, painted plaster. "Ramona Well" inscribed in base. 1930s. **$37.50.**

Herspanic (Hispanic) women and their jugs are reminiscent of ancient Greek symbolism – woman as *vessel/vassal*.

1. STATUETTE, 5 ³/₄" tall, painted plaster, "Marbello Artcraft Co. ©1952." **$12.50.**

2. STATUE, 12" tall, high-glaze ceramic, 1957. **$27.50.**

3. STATUE, 12" tall, semi-matte glaze in solid red. Same mold as #2. **$17.50.**

STATUE, 12" tall, painted plaster, signed "F. Lemuz Made in Mexico." Ever eager to dance and please, the *Herspanic* woman is attractive to *heterosexual white imperialist* males, as well as to her own señor. 1940s. **$35.**

African-American Women

1. VASE, 8" tall, ceramic. Appears to be a Nubian slave with a vessel to be used as a planter. 1940s. **$22.50.**

2. VASE, 6 1/2" tall, ceramic with fur. 1930s. **$27.50.**

3. VASE, 5 1/2" tall, ceramic, chartreuse with gold neck rings. 1950s. **!15.**

1

2

3

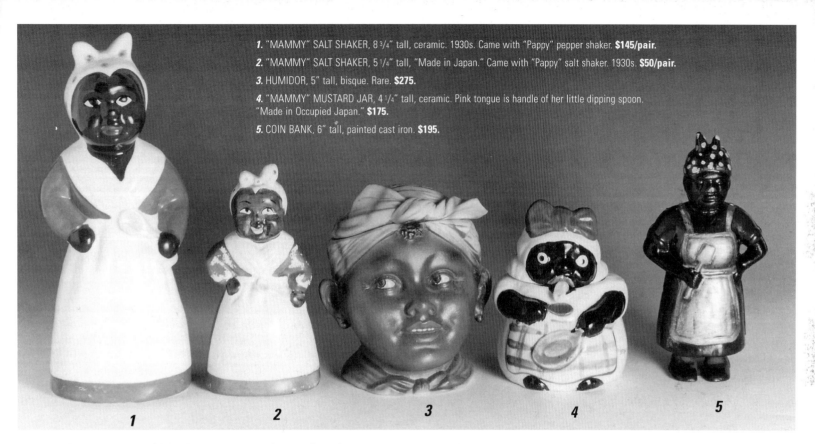

1. "MAMMY" SALT SHAKER, 8¾" tall, ceramic. 1930s. Came with "Pappy" pepper shaker. **$145/pair.**

2. "MAMMY" SALT SHAKER, 5¼" tall, "Made in Japan." Came with "Pappy" salt shaker. 1930s. **$50/pair.**

3. HUMIDOR, 5" tall, bisque. Rare. **$275.**

4. "MAMMY" MUSTARD JAR, 4¼" tall, ceramic. Pink tongue is handle of her little dipping spoon. "Made in Occupied Japan." **$175.**

5. COIN BANK, 6" tall, painted cast iron. **$195.**

1 *2* *3* *4* *5*

The portraits of black women are basically of two types: natives of Africa or Mammies. All black memorabilia brings a high price and is often collected by persons of African-American descent who have an ironic sense of humor. As found in advertising, memorabilia and objects associated with the kitchen, "Mammy" is usually seen positively and sometimes comically. The demand for black collectibles is so high that a great many of the "Mammy" objects are being reproduced.

173

Postcards, sheet music, and old advertising are rich sources of all kinds of politically incorrect stereotypes. Often you can get two-for-one, as in the case of these postcards from 1910–1960. Some of their intentions and humor is obscure today. As with other black collectibles, the demand is great so expect to pay $5–$50 for such material.

It's a toss up: which offense takes priority – racism, sexism, or in the use of dialect especially, classism?

NOTE: Sexism is not limited to blue eyed devils

Hula Hula Girls

SHEET MUSIC. Before Hollywood seized on the made-to-order media potential of the hula girl, Tin Pan Alley ground out numerous wacky songs featuring South Seas dancing girls. Reflecting the puritanical decorum of the audience of that period, much of this imagery is innocently flirtatious rather than overtly sexual. 1916. **$5-$8 each.**

CHALK CARNIVAL FIGURE, 11" tall, inscribed "Hula Hula" on base. This hula girl on a half shell is a Polynesian Venus. 1930s. **$125.**

While the hula girl is an *emergent* (member of an unrepresented identity group) *sun person* (person from a tropical clime), the popular image is not p.c. The Hawaiian hula girl with her undulating hips and swinging skirts is offensive to the sensibilities of *lookism* (idea that appearance is an indicator of a person's value) and *heterosexism* (oppression of sexual orientations other than heterosexual). She was attractive and she liked men. She was a fantasy come true for colonizing, Western, sea-faring men who envisioned mermaids in the seas they sailed, and found hula girls – like mermaids with legs – on the beach when they arrived.

"Back home at this time I'd be cuddled up with a good book."

COPR. 1944 EX. SUP. CO., CHGO., MADE IN U.S.A

Shore Leave

You love me, you love me not, you love me . . . !

COPR. 1941 EX. SUP. CO., CHGO., MADE IN U.S.A.

POSTCARDS, early 1940s. $3–$5/each.

1. CHALK CARNIVAL HULA GIRL, 16" tall. She flashes a Betty Boop–like wink. As the tourism industry began to pick up in the 1930s, many a hula girl's features became more European than native. 1930s. **$100.**

2. HULA GIRL LAMP, 24" tall, bronze-washed pot metal. Flip the switch once and the light turns on; again and a little motor in the base starts her hips swaying. We've seen about five versions. 1940s. Working lamps: **$600-$1,000.**

3. CHALK HULA GIRL, 12" tall. 1940s. **$90.**

4. SALT AND PEPPER SET, with hula girl in center. Ceramic. 1950s. **$15.**

5. PAIR OF FIGURINES, 4" tall, ceramic. Native Hawaiian couple in 1940s attire: he in Hawaiian shirt, she in muu-muu. Marked "Goertz Hawaii." 1940s. **$45/pair.**

6. PIN DISH, 2" tall. Bisque. "Made in Japan." 1950s. **$20.**

7. HULA DOLL, 7"tall, celluloid with eyes that open and close. 1950s. **$40.**

8. PAIR OF HULA GIRL FIGURINES, 6" tall, oil-painted, low-fired ceramic. Very detailed and more overtly sexual than the sheet music dancing beauties. 1940s. **$65/pair.**

HULA GIRL NOVELTY LAMP, 18 3/4" tall, wood, rope and fiber. Her breasts are lighted by Christmas bulbs in your choice of color. Another version has 2 hula girls and a palm tree. 1930s. **$275.**

An Emergent American Minority

A group particularly offensive to the multicultural sensitivities of the politically correct is the *mutant albino genetic-recessive global minority* (white people). If women are victims (and p.c. is, if anything, a virulent form of victimology) the ceremonies of American *women of non-color* should be pitied – but they're not. How infuriating then are the rituals of *melanin impoverished wimyn* (white women) such as beauty pageants and cheer-leading. *White skinned privilege* ain't what it used to be. Could it be that the p.c.ers have missed America?

1. STATUE, "MISS AMERICA," 15" tall, painted chalk carnival prize. 1940s. **$75.**

2. THERMOS, 6" tall, plastic. "Miss America" by Aladdin. Collectors buy and sell thermoses and lunchboxes separately. 1972. **$25.**

3. LUNCHBOX, painted metal. "Miss America" by Aladdin. All of the 24 contestants pictured are *ice princesses*, reflecting the lack of *appropriate diversity* in the dark ages before p.c. raised our consciousness. 1972. **$35.**

4. SOUVENIR BOTTLE, 9" tall, painted glass. Features the high points of Atlantic City, most importantly the "Miss America Pageant." 1966. **$28.**

Phallocentrism, as the politically correct realize, is that tendency of white males to indulge in testosterone-driven activities such as sports and war. Naturally, they enslave women into all manner of support services, especially in sexually provocative roles that further enflame the violent rituals of the *ego-testicle world view.*

1. CHALK CARNIVAL DRUM MAJORETTE, 15" tall. Marked "Illinois Plastic Products, St. Louis, MO." 1930s. **$75.**

2. MANTEL CLOCK, 11 ½" tall. Plated pot metal. Wind-up clock. 1940s. **$125.**

3. FIGURINE, 3" tall. Ceramic. "Made in Japan." 1950s. **$10.**

4. CHALK DRUM MAJORETTE, 13" tall. Drum majorettes come in many sizes and materials and range from coquettish and cute to skirt-bouncing pin up girls. 1940s. **$95.**

Tit & Cheekbone Determinism

The dominant white male paradigm posits a duty to beauty for women. "It is a social, cultural and economic fact that for some women their facial contours can determine their income and status more than their life chance situation. . . ."
— *Marjorie Ferguson, 1983*

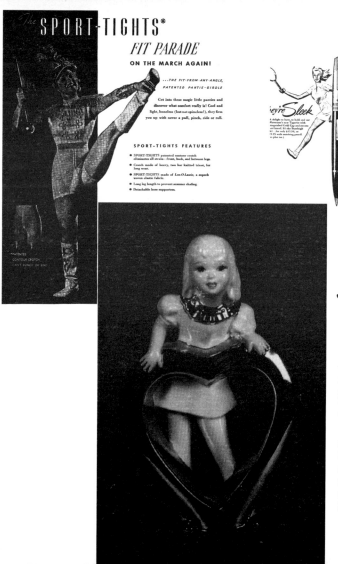

SWEETHEART FIGURINE, 6½" tall, glazed ceramic with gold heart, 1960s. **$18.**
This *prepubescent beauty-slave in training* (girl) may today have her consciousness raised when she learns from feminists that to be called a girl "is not so offensive on the surface as to be called a pig, yet the harm done may be deeper and longer-lasting." (Eve Merriam, 1974)

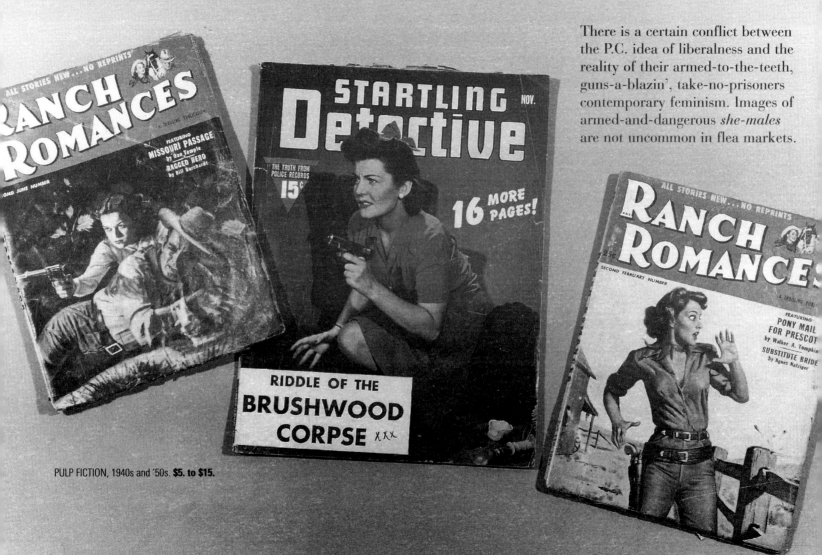

There is a certain conflict between the P.C. idea of liberalness and the reality of their armed-to-the-teeth, guns-a-blazin', take-no-prisoners contemporary feminism. Images of armed-and-dangerous *she-males* are not uncommon in flea markets.

PULP FICTION, 1940s and '50s. **$5. to $15.**

Culturally Challenged Women of Non Color

In this politically correct era there is only one ethnic group that we are aware of which it is still OK to ridicule: poor Southern whites (rednecks) and their hill-billy cousins. They are stereotyped as ignorant, barefoot, lazy, drunken, violent, and fecund. In some ways this contemporary imagery is more *nag-ative* than black stereotypes of the past. Aunt Jemima and Uncle Mose may have been domestics but at least they could hold a job.

DAISY MAE FIGURINE, 8" tall, polychromed composition, a souvenir of Dog Patch, U.S.A., a now-defunct Arkansas theme park based on Al Capp's comic strip. **$25.**

184

14. Politically Correct *Wofems*

Lest we leave the impression that **all** of the women's imagery of America's flea market treasures is politically incorrect, here are a few that should appeal to even the most critical feminist.

COW PRE-WOMEN FIGURINES, ceramic.

Left: 6¼" tall, Marked "Japan." 1950s. **$18**.

Right: 7" tall, "Made in *Western Imperialist Dominated* (Occupied) Japan." 1940s. **$28**.

An *Amazing Wild Woman Warrior* has just liberated a *phallocratic* ship of the line. She barks out the order: "I hear our prize has a cowardly cockswain by the name of Bobbitt cringing in the bilge. Well, bring Bobbitt to the poop deck for some *Sea-Hag* re-education. Har-har-har."

PIRATE GIRL STATUETTE, 10½" tall, polychromed brittania metal with bronze wash. 1920s. **$125**.

SHEET MUSIC from a
Broadway musical. **$5.**

Fighting Back

As these cartoons and postcards show, not all *wimmin* in *herstory* considered themselves victims. Comic postcards from 1910 to the 1950s are fairly common. Value ranges from **$1** to **$5**. Note the Irish slur in the cartoon from the early 1900s.

CARTOON FROM *JUDGE* MAGAZINE, August, 1925. **$17.50 per issue**

HE—*These comic men are all right, but, of course, they exaggerate things too much.*

SHE HAD THE WEIGHT.

PAT—"Shure, this is phwat a man gits fer marryin' out av his class."

MATCHBOOK, early 1950s. Illustration is a Petty painting. **$3.**

Halloween Fortune Wheel, 9 inches high. Witch and Fortune Wheel stands on a folding tissue base 6 inches in diameter. Spin the wheel and tell fortunes by the numbers. Fortunes are printed on two paddles that fold on the back and come out on either side with full directions, 2 dozen in box.

No. 99N89.
Per dozen... .75

HALLOWEEN FORTUNE WHEEL, 9" tall, die cut cardboard, 1931 **$42.50.**

HALLOWEEN DECORATIONS, embossed and decorated cardboard, 1931. **$18-$25.** Feminist hags are partial to black cats and owls. We don't know their disposition toward the political correctness of pumpkins.

ASSORTED HALLOWEEN DECORATION

188

Witches, Hags, Nags, Harpies, Spinsters, and Crones

. . . these are a few of her favorite things – Mary Daly, that is. With a deliciously tortured mixture of New Age paganism and old fashioned ball-busting, feminism's chief crone, Daly, has in her *Websters' First New Intergalactic Wickedary of the English Language* ridden the broomstick of radical feminism far into outer space. It has furnished us many hours of enjoyment. In witch-bitch Daly's own deconstructed English it is a "Guidebook for the Intergalactic Galloping of Nag-Gnostic Voyagers; Book of Guide Words for Wayward, Weirdward Wanderers." And you thought Halloween was just for trick-or-treaters!

UTENSIL HOLDER WITCH, 9¼" tall, low fired with spackled finish, 1950s. **$12.50.**

Witch, 18 inches high in full Hallowe'en colors, die-cut. Arms and legs are eyleted to body and are movable. Packed 1 dozen to box. **No. 99N4.** Per dozen.......... **.75**

WITCH, 18", die cut cardboard. 1931. **$37.50.**

STATUE, available in three sizes, 12", 21", and 29" in plaster (marketed as alabaster), 1889. Today's value **$175 to $375.** Aglaia, Thalia, and Euphrosyne, the Three Graces, a Victorian parlor piece that looks like *women-identified women* (lesbian goddesses) to us.

> *Spinsters* are *self-identified women* (lesbians) who "whirl in all directions away from the death march of patriarchy."

OIL PAINTING, 18" x 24" on canvas board, framed. Signed "Jack Deming," 1960s. **$50.** (NOTE: Really bad art is appreciating fast.)

The Ways of Women-Identified Women

When not flying reconnaissance on their broomsticks, crones gather in covens, spin up a storm, and make *pre-crones* (baby feminists). Having a baby the old-fashioned way involves way too much intimate contact with the *cockocracy* (patriarchal society of males) like fathers and doctors. *Baster Babies* are produced with sperm donated by a gay friend and insemi-nated with a turkey baster.

Element from a 1941 ad for *Ethyl* (lead), an antiknock fluid added to gasoline.

Cut from a 1911 temperance book. Truth has two Moms.

15. On Collecting P.I.C.

You now have permission to look at political incorrectness with curiosity and understanding, even with a smile. True, it may be trash stuff, but it's also a guilty pleasure, like a hot dog: Junk food for the soul. Sometimes nothing else will do. Relish it. A joke can be a way station on the road to the solution of a problem. The joke or the insulting/demeaning artifact often recognizes that the problem exists. How much can you trust people with *humor-deficit disorder* (HDD), the virus that seems to infect the politically correct?

America was a rough frontier and the people who made it here had rough ways. Still it cannot be said that they did not recognize the power of the female in all many of her various manifestations. Sexy, sacred, or saccharine, woman is an icon to behold, boldly portrayed in carnival chalks, pinups, corny advertising, lighters, ashtrays, and coffee cups. It is clear that American men are interested in but at times perplexed and confused about the object of their obsession. The evidence is on the shelves. So now, get thee to the flea markets, garage sales, household dispersals, and auctions and collect intelligently.

You may have to retrain your eye. Skip the bland, well-designed, tasteful, monochromatic household goods. Search out figural objects, things with faces, bright colors, awkward casting, grinning stereotypes. Remember that this was mostly mass produced and

it has blanketed the country evenly. From sprawling outdoor swap meets to little old lady glass and china shows, once you've sensitized yourself to the incorrect you can find it everywhere.

Specialty shows can be a bonanza. Toys are rife with gender stereotyping: tin battery-operated secretaries type away on little tin desks, girl-sized housekeeping tools and little pink refrigerators abound. Postcard and ephemera shows are loaded with imagery that should grate on P.C. sensibilities. Cookie jar and wall pocket dealers may not recognize what incorrectness they harbor on their tables. Older, middle-class dealers still can't focus on popular culture. What may appear to some to be a fusty, bourgeois glass and china show may yield treasures of seminude, plaster, classical statuary. Roseville pottery collectors may not be aware of the exploitative implications of the Silhouette line.

A lot of the material bears an uncanny resemblance to post-Modern art. Now that some of these poseurs, like Jeff Koons, are getting their tits in a copyright wringer for appropriating Jim Beam decanters, connoisseurs of chic kitsch may have to settle for the real thing: cheap kitsch. The game of provocative parallels got started when astute New York loft loungers noticed that African masks look like Cubist sculpture (Duh!) and Amish quilts looked like hard-edge abstract paintings (that one is a bit of a puzzle). Politically incorrect

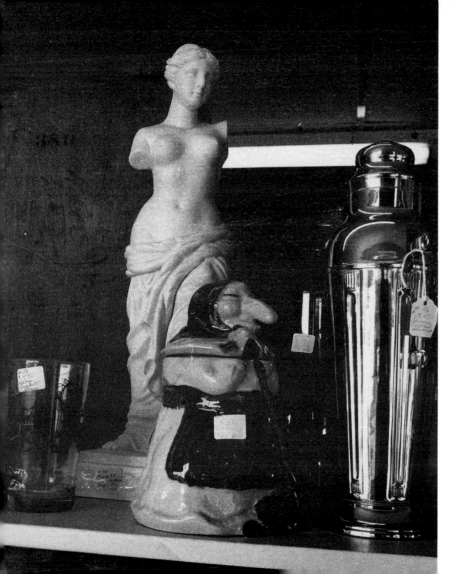

stuff can now serve a parallel, post-Modern, deconstructed decorating function for a lot less money.

There is a confounded mystery about artifacts, even ones of fairly recent vintage. Every time we set up as dealers at the Sunday flea market at 26th Street and 6th avenue we saw Andy Warhol and his entourage eyeballing the sea of stuff. Andy's genius may not have been in his art, a tad overblown and derivative for our taste, as much as it was in his passionate and serious attention to the power of flea market finds. He was one of the West's great collectors. He never shied away from a striking image, never looked at the pedigree or the bottom of a vase to judge its merit. Like the Surrealists of the 1920s, '30s, and '40s he recognized that powerful, captivating imagery is not the exclusive property of any one class.

Get reacquainted with your roots. Flea market people are on the cutting edge of commerce. They may be on the way up or on the way down. In America hard times are often the start of something big. They are trend seekers and trend setters. You'll find it in a flea market before you find it in a museum, if you can find a museum open in the future.

Bring along a folding table and chair and put out some of your own stuff to sell. When you sell something for more than you paid for it, you'll be proud of yourself – but don't quit your day job. To find out something's true worth, try to sell it. Don't completely trust price guides – even this one. In a free market things do change fast. We've been in on several gold

Kitsch, Camp, Bad Taste, and Political Correctness

Often used to characterize expressive but cheaply made goods, these terms, kitsch, camp, and bad taste, are excessively subjective and often condescending and leftist. The concepts also deny the raw power of much of the imagery. Even Susan Sontag admits the attraction/repulsion syndrome in her uncharacteristically apolitical and semilucid essay, *On Camp*.

Connoisseurs of the truly awful generally have a campy sensibility. They find a certain esthetic interest in the tawdry (black velvet paintings for instance) and the ridiculous and excessive: Liberace, Jayne Mansfield, leopard skin Spandex, and Dolly Parton's mammaries. Other bad taste phenomena are entertainments like Vegas, Roller Derby, Hulk Hogan, roadside dinosaur parks, and miniature golf. Bad taste collectibles are lava lamps, snow domes, and paint-by-number art. Pink poodles, tattoos, and Frederick's of Hollywood also can provide esthetic rewards. As with camp, the more unconscious the aberration or failure, the bigger the buzz the fans of bad taste get.

There is, of course, a measure of semantic overlap between Kitsch, Camp, and Slang Americana. All are products of mass culture and are often cheaply produced. The material

we're considering, Slang Americana, most often intends to produce a shock effect. Camp or Bad Taste are usually intended to be serious, beautiful, sentimental, or elegant, but fall far from achieving those goals. Slang Americana is often about gender or ethnicity, intentionally insulting, and like slang language (slanguage) it doesn't mess around with fussy style. It's cheap and expedient, like Kitsch. Of course, such slangy artifacts do possess many Bad Taste virtues, but they are not an accident.

SUFFRAGETTE VOTE-GETTING
THE EASIEST WAY.

rushes: patchwork quilts, scientific instruments, American Indian artifacts, robots, art deco. We collected TV lamps when we couldn't afford Staffordshire. The imagery is there for the taking. It can be an excellent adventure, and profitable.

To set the record straight, rest assured that we welcome the politically correct to search these artifacts out, too. If it proves your point, take it to class. Bid up the price, feminists.

We didn't collect this stuff or write this book just to infuriate antsy, authoritarian feminists. If we do, it'll just be a delightful side effect. As shadowy marginals on the fringes of the legit antiques trade we had to move farther and farther from authentically old stuff to deco then to '50s, as prices in each category rose, closing our profit margin. The final frontier we have found is what we are calling Politically Incorrect Collectibles or Slang Americana. Not being completely *intelligence-deprived* (stupid), we began to be aware of how intriguing and dangerous these little trinkets had become. If the brave new world gets bent out of shape over complimenting a woman on her new dress or an African NBA star promoting Uncle Ben's Rice, we began to wonder seriously what this country was coming to.

A final word of advice: Keep your collection at home and don't intentionally offend anyone. The truth may or may not set you free, but hopefully the truth won't get you fired. Have fun.

Kitsch Academia

Political correctness, a slurred pop descent of philosophy, was aided by progressively less-learned theorists who made intellectual castings of castings of castings, philosophical photocopies of photocopies of photocopies until recognition of the original theory was almost impossible. Somehow Einstein's brilliant physics is slurred into the relativistic behavior so embraced today by the P.C. University. Heisenberg's Theory of Indeterminacy is misapplied metaphysically to justify the absence of order and consistency in scholarship. Need one guess what these scientific illiterates with liberal arts Ph.D's have done with Chaos Theory?

No small part of the whiney tone of the politically correct comes from the fact that its proponents are baby boomers, a generation that grew up immersed in TV, mass media, suburbia and the socially engineered welfare state. It's no accident they are so inflamed by slang which is the product of an earlier, more individualistic American culture. Political correctness is itself a kind of Sixties kitsch, closely related to the various pop romantic student rebellions of the era. The mushy-headed, pinko student radicals of yore are now mushy-headed, tenured pinko professors.

THE OPPRESSED MINORITIES

It didn't bode well that kitschy left-wing popularizations hit the American education establishment when the multicultural, self esteem and victimization fads were beginning to assert the idea that standards of any kind were oppressive.

Not only do we not believe that the most cruel and satiric stereotypes are of much consequence in the larger arena of economics and politics, we really wonder if high art is of much political consequence either. The left has always had a love affair with didactic art.

The arrogance of the romantic artist shows through here: "the pen is mightier than the sword." To the wishful thinking of the wan, romantic artist, P.C. adds the totalitarians' equally unfounded faith in propaganda and media. But American politics and culture have roots deeper than the industrial age. You can get a consumer to buy a certain brand of candy bar through repetition and seductive advertising more easily than you can alter the content and direction of a society. Again, we think that the American people can survive this mixed record of sometimes savage humor better than they can the distortions of academic neologists or bureaucratic censors.

Sticks and stones may break my bones, but words can never hurt me" – and, may we add, neither can girlie matchbooks, comic postcards, or rude ashtrays.

Of all the preposterous aspects of political correctness perhaps the biggest *departure from verifiable reality* (lie) is that America singled out minorities for humorous ridicule. A quick perusal of the contents of humor books like this will reveal that nothing and no one are safe from the American slanguage's love of hyperbole, exaggeration, cutting observation, disdain for pomp and pretense and an all around hatred of tyranny. Immigrants (African-Americans excepted, of course) came to the New World to be free, and, by God, all of us *wannabe*. It was a bodacious, outrageous experiment and it ain't over till the *adipose-tissue-enhanced, larger than standard female vocalist performs* (the fat lady sings).

This is a cut from a circa-1900 humor book which reminds us that P.C. rhetoric has a snotty morally superior tone associated with the Puritans and reformers of the northeast United States. The earlier objectors to vernacular, or slang, had not, at that time, acquired Marxist methods of enforcement.

ANOTHER BOUT WITH BOSTON.

THAT BOSTON BOY (*bless him!*)—"Pardon me, but during the heated discussion you just held with your sister I heard you command her to 'stop chewing the rag.' Don't you think it would have been more gentlemanly to have said, 'Desist masticating the fabric'?"

Resources

First and foremost, check in with the Politically Incorrect Collectibles Association (P.I.C.A.), 3020 S. National, #340, Springfield, MO 65804. We have a newsletter that covers all areas of incorrectness (not just *wofems*), a groovy membership card and info on incorrect goings-on around the country. All in the spirit of good clean satiric fun.

Books and magazines about antiques and collectibles fill the bookstores. In the last five years or so there has been an explosion of information on even the narrowest of collecting topics. There are specialty newsletters and periodicals on postcards and ephemera, toys, wall pockets, Happy Meal collectibles, and lots more. Some publications, like the *Maine Antique Digest*, P.O. Box 645, Waldoboro, ME and *The Antique Trader*, P.O. Box 1050, Dubuque, IA, are available only by subscription, but many libraries do subscribe.

Many antiques malls carry a wide range of these narrow-focus collecting publications.

Today many antiques shows are themed around a period, style, or type of material. There are shows devoted to art deco, art pottery, advertising, toys, dolls, head vases, wall pockets, guns, Indian material, even shows devoted entirely to matchbooks. Auctions can be devoted to a single type of material: taxidermy, for instance, or gambling or arrowheads.

Some collectors concentrate on a single theme (holidays perhaps), personality ("Everything Elvis"), or style. Politically Incorrect material can be found in almost every category, if you just look at them in a new and more *sensitive* light. Therefore you are free to raid other categories looking for your chosen "incorrect" collectibles be it girlie, racial, ethnic, or animal rights.

AMERICAN MADE & POLITICALLY INCORRECT

Acknowledgments

We owe special thanks to our editor, Jim Fitzgerald, who not only took on this project, but exhorted us to "take 'em on, don't hold back, put it all in." His assistant, Regan Good, kept track of him and kept us on track.

John Margolies continues to be an amazement and an inspiration to us.

Jim Hawkins's design and layout added real punch to the pages.

Here in the Midwest we found much cheerful cooperation with the project. Collectors lent us treasured items to photograph. Mall and shop owners would allow us to bring lights in and photograph merchandise from many booths. Antique show managers let us set up in the corner and dealers let us take things from their booths to photograph.

Thanks especially to Mike and Carol Cochran, connoisseurs of pinup art, and Randy Ebrite, Mike's partner in Nellie Dunn's, an antique emporium in Springfield. They were generous with rare collectibles as well as their time, photo space and merchandise. Other shops we'd like to thank are Park Central Flea Market, Perry's General Store, Maine Streete Mall, and Ozark Antique Mall.

About the Authors:

Leland and Crystal Payton are the founders and C.E.O.s of P.I.C.A. (the Politically Incorrect Collectibles Association). Leland Payton is a recovering nature photographer and watercolorist. His hillbilly heritage (they've been called the most deliberately unprogressive people in the world) goes far in explaining his retrograde attitudes.

Crystal's deviations from feminist agendas may be explained by years of brainwashing by Visitation nuns and Jesuit priests: notorious *propagandists of patriarchy*. In her spare time she enjoys cooking, cleaning, and beating the laundry out on the rocks for her guys.

They live in Springfield, MO, with their two teenage sons, Strader and Ross, who got much of their book larnin' from *MAD* magazine. The boys already show symptoms of testosterone-poisoning: Strader is a kickboxer whose favorite subject is Japanese and Ross is a U.S. Navy Sea Cadet who spends his spare time surfing the Internet.